"Hooray to Randolph and Posner for simplifying the complicated process of managing projects successfully!"

— STEVE CARTER
President
Carter Goble Lee

"*Checkered Flag Projects* is a winner that will quickly get your project teams to the finish line with a common language, effective process, and useful tools. This workbook will be especially useful for multidisciplinary teams whose members have a diverse range of experience in project management."

— ROBERT L. PHILLIPS
President & CEO
Guide Dogs for the Blind, Inc.

"*Checkered Flag Projects* is an eminently practical guide for organizing and executing projects. Especially useful were the sections on mobilizing, motivating, and managing people in the process."

— JEFFREY B. SAMET
Vice President and Principal
Colliers Pinkard

"*Checkered Flag Projects* provides the answers and much more—an insightful guide and reference for projects in any profession, and an excellent resource for effective leadership."

— G. MICHAEL PERRY
Chief Human Resources Officer
DuPont Electronic Technologies

"Fact-based decision making, a robust process, cross-functional team building, and ways to manage what's right, not who's right—a recipe for success for project management. It's all there for anyone who is managing one project or who does project management for a living."

— BOB CECIL
Senior Business Consultant
General Management Technologies

"Finally, an enlightened approach to project management that recognizes the importance of people and provides extraordinary insight on leading teams through winning projects. Required reading for all types of managers."

— KARL HAMLIN
President and CEO
K.S. Hamlin & Associates

"Motivation, passion, conflicts—*Checkered Flag Projects* addresses how to focus this energy toward project goals. An outstanding guide to building and empowering a winning team."

— JOHN T. DONNELLY
President
IntePro Solutions

"The rules in this easy-to-read road map for successful projects are so helpful—a must read for anyone who has had difficulty crossing the finish line with their projects."

— JENNIFER STANFORD
Director of Professional Development
Robbins Gioia, LLC

"This is a good read and a long-lasting resource. Posner and Randolph hit the mark, creating an understanding that project management is a dynamic, team-oriented enterprise. This can change the way you manage work."

— CHUCK WHITE
President
Sigma Phi Epsilon Educational Foundation

"I'm a big fan of Randolph and Posner's approach. Their practical ideas can help any manager do a better job."

— LINDA WILSHUSEN
Executive Director
Santa Cruz County Regional Transportation Commission

CHECKERED FLAG
PROJECTS

Second Edition

ISBN 0-13-009399-8

90000

9 780130 093998

Financial Times Prentice Hall Books

For more information, please go to www.ft-ph.com

Thomas L. Barton, William G. Shenkir, and Paul L. Walker
Making Enterprise Risk Management Pay Off:
How Leading Companies Implement Risk Management

Deirdre Breakenridge
Cyberbranding: Brand Building in the Digital Economy

William C. Byham, Audrey B. Smith, and Matthew J. Paese
Grow Your Own Leaders: How to Identify, Develop, and Retain
Leadership Talent

Jonathan Cagan and Craig M. Vogel
Creating Breakthrough Products: Innovation from Product Planning
to Program Approval

Subir Chowdhury
The Talent Era: Achieving a High Return on Talent

Sherry Cooper
Ride the Wave: Taking Control in a Turbulent Financial Age

James W. Cortada
21st Century Business: Managing and Working
in the New Digital Economy

James W. Cortada
Making the Information Society: Experience, Consequences,
and Possibilities

Aswath Damodaran
The Dark Side of Valuation: Valuing Old Tech, New Tech,
and New Economy Companies

Henry A. Davis and William W. Sihler
Financial Turnarounds: Preserving Enterprise Value

Sarv Devaraj and Rajiv Kohli
The IT Payoff: Measuring the Business Value
of Information Technology Investments

Jaime Ellertson and Charles W. Ogilvie
Frontiers of Financial Services: Turning Customer Interactions
Into Profits

Nicholas D. Evans
Business Agility: Strategies for Gaining Competitive Advantage
through Mobile Business Solutions

Kenneth R. Ferris and Barbara S. Pécherot Petitt
  Valuation: Avoiding the Winner's Curse

David Gladstone and Laura Gladstone
  *Venture Capital Handbook: An Entrepreneur's Guide
  to Raising Venture Capital, Revised and Updated*

David R. Henderson
  The Joy of Freedom: An Economist's Odyssey

Philip Jenks and Stephen Eckett, Editors
  *The Global-Investor Book of Investing Rules: Invaluable Advice
  from 150 Master Investors*

Thomas Kern, Mary Cecelia Lacity, and Leslie P. Willcocks
  *Netsourcing: Renting Business Applications and Services
  Over a Network*

Frederick C. Militello, Jr., and Michael D. Schwalberg
  Leverage Competencies: What Financial Executives Need to Lead

Dale Neef
  E-procurement: From Strategy to Implementation

John R. Nofsinger
  *Investment Madness: How Psychology Affects Your Investing…
  And What to Do About It*

Tom Osenton
  *Customer Share Marketing: How the World's Great Marketers Unlock
  Profits from Customer Loyalty*

W. Alan Randolph and Barry Z. Posner
  *Checkered Flag Projects: 10 Rules for Creating and Managing Projects
  that Win, Second Edition*

Stephen P. Robbins
  The Truth About Managing People…And Nothing but the Truth

Eric G. Stephan and Wayne R. Pace
  *Powerful Leadership: How to Unleash the Potential in Others
  and Simplify Your Own Life*

Jonathan Wight
  Saving Adam Smith: A Tale of Wealth, Transformation, and Virtue

Yoram J. Wind and Vijay Mahajan, with Robert Gunther
  *Convergence Marketing: Strategies for Reaching
  the New Hybrid Consumer*

CHECKERED FLAG PROJECTS

10 RULES FOR CREATING AND MANAGING PROJECTS THAT WIN!

Second Edition

W. Alan Randolph
University of Baltimore

Barry Z. Posner
Santa Clara University

FINANCIAL TIMES
Prentice Hall

An Imprint of Pearson Education
Upper Saddle River, NJ · London · New York · San Francisco · Toronto
Sydney · Tokyo · Singapore · Hong Kong · Cape Town
Madrid · Paris · Milan · Munich · Amsterdam

Library of Congress Cataloging-in-Publication Data
Randolph, W. Alan.
    Checkered flag projects : 10 rules for creating and managing projects that win / W. Alan Randolph,
    Barry Z. Posner.—2nd edition.
        p. cm.
    Includes bibliographical references and index.
    ISBN 0-13-009399-8
        1. Project management. I. Posner, Barry Z. II. Title.

    T56.8.R36 2002
    658.4'04--dc21

Editorial/Production Supervision: *Faye Gemmellaro*
Executive Editor: *Jim Boyd*
Editorial Assistant: *Allyson Kloss*
Marketing Director: *Bryan Gambrel*
Manufacturing Buyer: *Maura Zaldivar*
Cover Designer: *Design Source*
Cover Design Director: *Jerry Votta*
Interior Design: *Meg VanArsdale*
Art Director: *Gail Cocker-Bogusz*

© 2002 and 1992 by Pearson Education, Inc.
Published by Prentice Hall PTR
Upper Saddle River, New Jersey 07458

Previously published as *Getting the Job Done! Managing Project Teams and Task Forces for Success.*

Prentice Hall books are widely used by corporations and government agencies for training, marketing, and resale.

For information regarding corporate and government bulk discounts, please contact:

Corporate and Government Sales, (800) 382-3419, or corpsales@pearsontechgroup.com

Printed in the United States of America

10   9   8   7   6   5   4   3   2   1

ISBN 0-13-009399-8

Pearson Education Ltd.
Pearson Education Australia PTY, Ltd.
Pearson Education Singapore, Pte. Ltd.
Pearson Education North Asia Ltd.
Pearson Education Canada, Ltd.
Pearson Educación de Mexico, S.A. de C.V.
Pearson Education—Japan
Pearson Education Malaysia, Pte. Ltd.

Dedicated to Our Wives
Ruth Anne and Jackie
for Their Continuous
Love and Friendship

Contents

About the Authors

W. Alan Randolph is Professor of Management at the Robert G. Merrick School of Business at the University of Baltimore, Baltimore, Maryland. He is also a senior consulting partner with The Ken Blanchard Companies in Escondido, California.

Alan is an internationally recognized consultant and trainer in such areas as project management, empowerment, high-performing teams, leadership, and performance management. As a consultant, seminar presenter, and speaker, he is relaxed, clear, and to the point.

Alan has published in a variety of practitioner and academic journals, including, among others, *Organizational Dynamics*, *Sloan Management Review*, and *Harvard Business Review*. His recent books include the best-selling *Empowerment Takes More Than a Minute* (2nd ed., 2001) and *The 3 Keys to Empowerment: Release the Power within People for Astonishing Results* (1999), both written with Ken Blanchard and John P. Carlos.

Barry Z. Posner is Professor of Leadership and Dean at the Leavey School of Business at Santa Clara University, Santa Clara, California.

Barry is an internationally recognized scholar and educator who has received both his school's and his university's highest faculty awards. He is a sought-after presenter and speaker who is dynamic and inspiring.

Barry has published widely in both practitioner and academic journals, including, among others, *Academy of Management Journal*, *Journal of Applied Psychology*, and *IEEE Transactions in Engineering Management*. He has also written several best-selling books, most recently *The Leadership Challenge* (3rd ed., 2002) and *Encouraging the Heart: A Leader's Guide to Rewarding and Recognizing Others* (1999), both written with James M. Kouzes.

Acknowledgments

No authors can write a practical project management book like this one without help, insight, and support from a number of people who work with projects every day. We owe a deep debt of gratitude to the many people with whom we have consulted over the years on the topic of Project Planning and Management. They have told us about projects that crashed and burned, as well as projects that got the coveted checkered flag. And it is from these experiences that we have been able to distill the 10 rules for creating and managing projects that win.

A special thanks goes to the following colleagues who have been especially instrumental in our learning and writing process as we have worked with them in business settings. You have our sincere thanks and appreciation for your insights, caring, and encouragement.

Patricia West, Kevin Duffy, and Dara Engelhardt with
  Pricewaterhouse Coopers, LLP

Mark Robbins, Jennifer Stanford, and David Heckman with
  Robbins Gioia, Inc.

Stephen Carter with Carter, Goble Associates

John Donnelly with IntePro Solutions

Mike Perry with E. I. DuPont, Corp.

Jeff Samet with Colliers, Pinkard, Inc.

George Summerson with Hoechst Pharmaceutical, Inc.

Marvin Jones with Inland Container Corp.

Alan Schneider with the Federal Communications Commission

We also wish to thank a number of consulting and educational colleagues from whom we have learned so much, as we have jointly pursued research, writing, and education projects:

Ken Blanchard, John Carlos, Pat Zigarmi, Drea Zigarmi, Don
  Carew, and Eunice Parisi-Carew with The Ken Blanchard
  Companies

Karl Hamlin with K. S. Hamlin & Associates

Peter Grazier with TeamBuilding, Inc.

Dennis Pitta with the University of Baltimore

Jim Kouzes, author and leadership consultant

In addition, we wish to express special thanks to our daughters, Ashley, Shannon, Liza, and Amanda, who have taught us so much about getting to the checkered flag. And we would be remiss not to recognize the support, encouragement, and guidance provided by our wives, Ruth Anne and Jackie. We could not have done this work without each of you being in our lives.

Finally, this book project has been a challenging race for us as authors who were guided by a desire to provide an outstanding tool for project leaders. We have worked together and followed the 10 rules for ourselves. The wonderful support we have received from the staff at Financial Times–Prentice Hall has been outstanding. Special thanks go to our editor, Jim Boyd, and to our previous editor, Bernard Goodwin. They have been a part of our team from start to finish, as have many others at FT–PH. We think we have managed to get the checkered flag and hope our readers will agree.

Thanks again to everyone cited above. You are dear and special people in our lives.

W. Alan Randolph   *Barry Z. Posner*
Baltimore, Maryland   Santa Clara, California

Introduction

Effective management of projects has become an essential part of the game in business today. Project work affects and engages almost everyone who works. As a consequence, speed, quality, and cost have taken on combined and interactive significance in the worlds of both business and government. In this environment, both challenge and opportunity await project leaders. Each project is like a race to be won or lost. We like to relate this to driving in a car race, where the symbol of winning is the checkered flag. Thus, "checkered flag projects" is the metaphor we will use for projects that win—that is, ones that are completed on time, within budget, and with high quality.

The questions for each project leader are "Am I prepared for this role?" and "What can I do to be more successful with projects?" In short, "How can I be the leader of checkered flag projects?" As you consider these general questions, we invite you to also ponder the more specific questions below:

1. Do you always know what the end result of your project work will look like?

2. Do the end users of your project ever change their minds about what they want? And if so, can you deal with these changes effectively?

3. Do your projects require you to finish assignments by a specified, and short, deadline?

4. Do you always seem to have multitask work that involves multiple people?

5. Do your projects have to be completed with a limited set of resources?

6. Do you have to work with people in other business units and even other companies to get work done?

7. Do you regularly deal with conflicts about project work?

8. Do you have to somehow get people on a team to be creative and motivated?

If you answered yes to even a few of these questions, you are squarely in the challenging world of projects. Nowadays, regardless of job title, almost every manager has responsibilities for project work, at least some of the time. It is clearly time to learn how to plan and manage projects for more success and better results with greater ease. Are you ready to become a leader of checkered flag projects? A leader of projects that win?

If you answered yes to these questions, this book is written for you. For the last 20 years, we have been providing seminars and consulting services on Project Planning and Management throughout the world. We have learned a great deal from studying hundreds of projects in a variety of organizational settings. We have also learned from the actual experiences of thousands of people who manage and work on all kinds of projects. Through our discussions with managers and our studies of projects and the teams that do the work, we have distilled ten key rules for project success—what we like to refer to as rules for creating and managing "checkered flag projects."

By reading this book, you will pick up proven ideas that will save you time, aggravation, and money. You will learn how to build a **GOCART** plan for your race and how to Supercharge that plan. You will also learn about the skills a **DRIVER** needs to get the coveted checkered flag!

Checkered Flag Projects can help you create and manage winning projects. It can make you a more successful project leader. We wish you well in learning to deal effectively with both the challenge and the opportunity that projects afford. Are you ready to become a consistent leader of "checkered flag projects"? If so, then let the race begin!

Managing Projects: Challenge and Opportunity

*Projects have become the essence of work; a project
leader must develop the skills to be a winner!*

The world of work has been forever changed. The Internet, technological
innovation, globalization, and dynamic customer needs provide businesses with constant challenges and opportunities. The very nature of work
has been shifted from daily activity to the exciting world of projects. The
life cycle of products and services is so much shorter that leaders must
continually initiate new ideas just to stay in the game. And dealing with
initiation, development, and utilization means you are dealing in the world
of projects. You must generate ideas and convert them into quality new
products and services in real time and in profitable ways. Otherwise, you
will be out of business. We have entered an era that calls for a change in
the way we manage work in organizations.

No longer will a hierarchical organizational structure, and the limiting
mindset that accompanies it, yield quality new ideas that are implemented in a timely fashion, within budget, and with no defects. No longer will
a functional approach to work promote and facilitate the kind of innovation, experimentation, and entrepreneurship that is needed if you want to
survive, much less excel. Nothing short of a radical shift to horizontally

oriented, fluid, project-focused organizations will be effective. You must become a project leader of renown, a winner, or by default you will become a loser! In a race, people recall the name of the winner, not of the fifth place, third place, or even the second place finisher.

The competitive battlefront for organizations is now defined by:

- Speed to market with new innovative ideas

- Superior customer service

- Lean and tight organization budgeting

To achieve a competitive advantage, indeed, to even remain a contender in this new race, means you must focus your energies on being innovative, while maintaining the highest-quality standards, getting work done more quickly, and controlling costs. What many organizations have begun to realize is that these outcomes can only be accomplished by people who feel empowered to use their minds and hearts and who are organized into empowered project teams.

Pioneering companies like Microsoft, General Electric, Intel, Ford, Springfield Remanufacturing Company, and Semco (in Brazil), to name only a few, have demonstrated significant increases in innovation and profitability by using empowered project teams that are designed and planned to tap the real potential and motivation of people. By organizing around project teams that are created to focus on problems and opportunities and then are dissolved when the job is done, leaders instill a sense of entrepreneurship, ownership, and engagement throughout their organizations.

The effective leaders of these project teams draw upon the experience, knowledge, and internal motivation of all team members and integrate these sources of power with the power of project management techniques and technology to create a powerful synergy. New ideas are generated and people become passionate about making their ideas work. Implementation succeeds with blinding speed and with high quality and low costs as essential complements.

More than ever, successful leadership means
being an effective project leader.

Successfully leading projects is the essential skill for managers today. To lead in the global, high tech, complex world of business means working effectively across disciplines, focusing people's attentions on a shared, inspirational purpose, maintaining a presence even when absent, and being able to strike a balance between flexibility and planning. Every successful manager will be a *project team leader*—regardless of conventional title, level, or job description. In this book we show you how to become a project leader who wins. Specifically, we help you better understand the challenges of projects and some powerful rules to guide your efforts in becoming a project leader who routinely comes away with the checkered flag—the symbol of a winner!

Becoming an Effective Project Leader

To excel at this new management challenge, you must view yourself as a leader with little organizational authority but with significant responsibility and significant powers to get the job done. The traditional functional manager relies on position power and predictable work flows. A project leader relies on empowerment of the team and new work patterns created for the moment. To become an exceptional project leader, you must think and work with a focus on innovation and empowered teams formed for a specific, temporary purpose. You must begin to think of work as batched into a series of projects that have common characteristics but that are unique in focus. You need to appreciate that project-oriented work has the following characteristics, all of which make projects difficult and challenging to complete effectively:

1. A unique, one-time focus

2. A specific need or problem to address

3. A starting point and a finish line

4. A time frame for completion

5. An ad hoc, cross-functional team

6. A limited set of shared resources

7. A sequencing of interdependent activities

8. An end user of the final deliverable

Effective project leaders understand these aspects of projects and how they contribute to numerous problems in getting the job done. Still, exceptional project leaders make things happen, but they do not do it alone. More than just powerful leaders, they are enablers of the power of others.

The bottom line is that they get the job of innovation done *on time, within budget, and with high quality*. So, what is the secret to their success?

Part of the secret is how they visualize what must be done in project work. They know how to create a dedication and passion that encompasses the entire project team and all stakeholders. Exceptional project leaders help everyone distinguish between "a day at work" and what Tom Peters calls "a WOW project" (what we would call a "checkered flag" project). Some of the distinctions are as follows:

A Day at Work	A WOW Project
A job	A performance
Putting in time	An act of unbridled passion
Forgettable	Memorable
Numbing	Exhausting
Tepid	Hot
Ho-hum	It matters
Risk-averse	Adventuresome
Hidden	Exposed
Another day older	A growth experience

You may be asking, "How do they make this transition, how do they create a fabulous experience in their projects?" Such transition in the minds of people is not easy, but in this book we help you understand some of the skills and techniques by which you can create this passion. Below is a brief overview of what exceptional project leaders do, followed by a summary of the rules that capture their actions and that form the basis for this book.

One key idea to remember is that effective project leaders take the time necessary (time the rest of us say we do not have) to plan their projects with all stakeholders and with their team and to manage that plan well. Too often, ineffective project leaders try to complete a project without a well-designed plan. They operate with a "Let's fix it in the field" mentality, so it should come as no surprise when they encounter huge, unexpected problems that "blow the project out of the water." Effective project leaders appreciate the need to go slow at first, so they can go fast later. Because no project ever goes 100 percent according to plan, going slow at first enables the team to have a better idea about what to do when things go astray. Good planning leads to *smaller* problems during implementation, which facilitates "going faster later."

A second major idea to know is that effective project leaders involve a large number of people in the planning process. They also involve these people in answering a lot of risk assessment and contingency questions like: "What if this happens?" and "What could go wrong?" They anticipate problems and disagreements and take steps to build powerful agreements out of these conflicts. They build a strong sense of commitment and passion in all team members. They make certain that everyone involved in the project, people from across functions and organizational layers, is "signed up" and motivated to make the project succeed. They keep people informed and involved throughout the implementation process, continually soliciting inputs and suggestions.

A third major idea is that effective project leaders know when to stop planning and move into action. They have developed a sense for when the planning phase has exhausted the "What if?" questions (at least for now). And they understand how to help team members find a common ground, enabling project participants to work through their inevitable disagreements.

> *Effective project leaders know the importance of planning;*
> *they also know when to move into action.*

During implementation, effective project leaders employ their power to facilitate the application of the project team's power to push the project through to completion. They know how to develop credibility with their constituents and how to unleash everyone's creative energies and focus these energies on getting the job done.

Learning the 10 Rules for Creating and Managing Checkered Flag Projects

The rules for success in project work can be clearly articulated, and *no* project team will be successful if they do not follow these rules. Each rule provides a particular focal point for project leaders, but it is the holistic application of all 10 rules that generates the real power for driving to the checkered flag.

Below we briefly list the 10 rules for creating and managing checkered flag projects. The remaining chapters of the book explore each rule in detail.

1. Clarify the project **<u>G</u>oal**.

2. Use **<u>O</u>bjectives** to define responsibilities.

3. Establish **<u>C</u>heckpoints, <u>A</u>ctivities, <u>R</u>elationships, and <u>T</u>ime Estimates**.

4. **<u>S</u>upercharge** the plan with a picture.

5. **<u>D</u>evelop** an empowered project team.

6. **<u>R</u>einforce** people's motivation and energy.

7. **<u>I</u>nform** everyone regularly.

8. **<u>V</u>italize** people with energy from conflicts.

9. **<u>E</u>mpower** yourself and others.

10. **<u>R</u>isk** being creative.

The underlined letters of the boldfaced words in the first four rules spell **GOCART-S**. This is our acronym for building a supercharged project plan. Effective project leaders build a solid plan for each project: a **GOCART** which they **S**upercharge to get a **GOCART-S**. They then drive this vehicle from the start of the race to the finish line.

But even the best-built **GOCART-S** will not produce a winner without a skillful **DRIVER**. And that's what the underlined letters in the last six rules spell. This is our acronym for what needs to happen as you implement your plan, not necessarily in any particular order but as required in the life of the project. And when you know both how to build an effective project **GOCART-S** and how to use the skills required to be a successful **DRIVER**, you can not only drive your projects over the finish line but you can be the winner who receives the coveted "checkered flag."

As we explain the 10 rules for project success in the remainder of this book, you learn how to put into practice the rules for building your project **GOCART-S** and for developing your skills as a project **DRIVER**. That is, you learn (or relearn) how to master the rules needed to get the job done in the world of project teams. In short, you learn how to be a *Checkered Flag Project Leader*!

Rule One: Clarify the Project Goal

Goal setting takes time and energy, but you can't be successful without a compelling project goal.

The extremely critical first step in building supercharged **GOCART-S** for each of your projects is to set a clear and compelling **G**oal. What is the desired end result of your project? What problem will this project solve? What need will it fill? How will this project change the way we do our business? Amazingly, many people managing in a project environment cannot readily answer these questions! Consider the result of this lack of knowledge. As illustrated in the famous example from *Alice in Wonderland* (see Figure 1.1), "If you don't know where you're going, any road will get you there (somewhere, but where)!"

To succeed in a project, you must mentally start at the finish . . . and work backward. The clearer you are about the end result of your project, even though it may change, the more effectively you can plan the best way to achieve it.

Ever worked a jigsaw puzzle? You've got a thousand pieces to the puzzle—all the necessary resources to complete the project. How do you begin? By looking at the cover of the puzzle box and studying the picture of what the pieces will look like once they are assembled properly. In

---

From *Alice in Wonderland*

"Cheshire Puss," she began, rather timidly, as she did not at all know whether it would like the name: however, it only grinned a little wider. "Come, it's pleased so far," thought Alice, and she went on. "Would you tell me, please, which way I ought to go from here?"

"That depends a good deal on where you want to get to," said the Cat.

"I don't much care where—" said Alice.

"Then it doesn't matter which way you go," said the Cat.

"—so long as I get somewhere," Alice added as an explanation.

"Oh, you're sure to do that," said the Cat, "If you only walk long enough."

Figure 1.1 Without a Goal, You May Never Get There

other words, you start at the end result and plan backward to the beginning. Then you begin to work toward the final goal you have defined.

And since most projects require the involvement of other people, you must be able to articulate this clear project goal to all stakeholders and team members if they are to help you succeed. If the project team lacks a clear goal, even excellent skills and the best equipment will not be sufficient to ensure the team's success.

For example, suppose you gave a highly skilled archer the best equipment available and told her to start shooting, but did not tell her where the target was. The archer would have to shoot the arrows where she thinks is appropriate, but this would likely not be at the target you had in mind (Figure 1.2). It's not that the archer isn't trying; she just does not know where to aim. She soon winds up frustrated in her efforts, and you are disappointed in the results. Time and energy are wasted. The archer has wasted her expertise and the money you spent for her fine equipment. Whose fault is this? *Yours*, because you did not clarify the goal, nor did you empower the archer to ask questions to gain clarification.

If you don't point people in the right direction, if you don't give them the big picture (for instance, showing them the picture on the jigsaw puzzle box), if you can't get them to imagine how they would feel using the product or service (the end result of your project), you are locked into an activity trap! People will be busy spinning their wheels, but nothing significant will be accomplished. Your team may have all the skills and equipment needed for the project, but they will fail because they don't

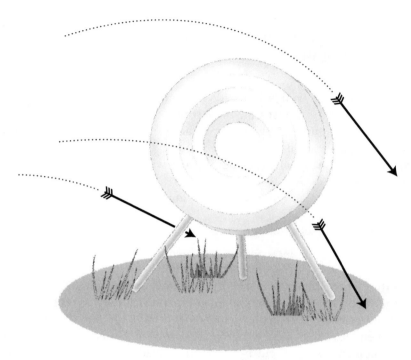

Figure 1.2 No Bull's-Eye for an Expert Archer Without a Clear Target

know where the target is and do not feel responsible for helping define the target.

But there is even more to the task of setting an overall project goal. Without emotion, passion, and commitment to the goal, team members will fall into the "day at work" mindset discussed in the previous chapter. No matter how mundane the project may seem, it is your job as project leader to reframe the project and continue reframing it until you and every member of the team feels a passion to get the job done. You, the team members, and the end user need to feel that the project has real, significant, and compelling meaning. The questions to ask yourself are "How can we feel a tremendous sense of pride at the end of this project?" and "How can we scope this project so the end user will become a Raving Fan of our team and its work?". Until you, the team members, and the stakeholders feel a burning passion for the project, keep working to reframe the goal until that passion is sparked.

Do not pass the start line of the project race until everyone feels a burning desire to get to the finish line in first place.

Setting Project Goals That Are Clear and Compelling

Many managers, as well as those in upper management, think it is easy to set goals for a project: just state them. But it is not easy. It's hard work. It is also the most important action you can take at the beginning of a project's life. What does it take to set a good project goal? What are the criteria of an effective goal, and what process will yield the clarity and passion you need?

In setting a project goal, you are trying to do two things:

1. Focus yourself, your end user, and your team on the target.

2. Create agreement, commitment, and energy for the project goal.

From where does this clarity of focus and energy come?

Ineffective project leaders often complain that they cannot get direction from customers or upper management. We have often heard people say that end users can state what they do *not* want, but not *what* they want. This statement is a cop-out by the project leader. When the goal is not clear, you must lead the end user through a process of goal clarification. And it is this process that takes time, energy, and *dialogue*. It is a process that involves conversation and discussion with the end user as you work toward a clarity of direction for the project. It is a process built on listening, dreaming big, and involving a significant number of people.

Since each project is to varying degrees unique—not something that has been done before—it is difficult to be clear on a goal right away. And since goal setting is a process of dialogue, it can start in one of two ways:

1. End users can tell you what they want.

2. You can tell the end users what you understand is the goal for the project.

Print it out on paper and personally show it to the end user while you say, "Here, this is what I think your project goal is. Have I got it right?" This gives the end user the option to say, "Yes, I agree. That's correct. Proceed." Or "No, that's not what I meant. Here's what I meant." As you go back and forth in this dialogue, you move closer and closer to achieving clarity about the direction and end result of the project. Too many project leaders feel they do not have time for this kind of dialogical goal-setting process. Yet it is amazing how many seem to find the time to correct the problems that result from poor goal clarity!

The best way to capture the project goal is in a statement of project results: How will we know we are finished? What will the end result look like? What will be different or better about the way we do our business? Effective project leaders do this by stating their goals in user terms. Think about this for a moment. Who is the user of your project? What does your user—client, customer, account, patient, or manager—want from you? What does the end user want this project to "fix"?

A user doesn't care, for example, that you are trying to produce a new accounting system (one ineffective way to describe a project's goal). The user cares about obtaining certain information about inventory and sales at the end of the day. Providing a system that meets the user's needs is your goal; designing a new accounting system is your process for doing this. Putting yourself on the user's side improves your chances of hitting the target.

In fact, if you do not define the goal in the end user's terms, the project may be done for the wrong reasons. For example, an information system was installed at a teaching hospital to provide the faculty with patient information for medical research purposes. Every faculty member was provided a personal computer tied to a network for access to the data. When the system was installed, no one could understand why the faculty did not use it. Hospital administrators wanted the system installed because they thought it would help the faculty with their research. Since they were the ones who made the contract with the consultants and paid the bills, they were perceived as the end user. But, in fact, the faculty members were the true end users, and they were never consulted about the system. A great system was installed, but it did not consider the needs of the actual end users. It failed miserably!

Setting a project goal requires a two-way dialogue with the end user to create clarity and buy-in.

But lest you move too quickly, you must consider how to involve the team members in this dialogue as early as possible. This can sometimes be difficult because the team may not yet be identified or "signed on to" the project. But don't let that stop you from expanding the conversation to include others in your organization. You need perspective from as many team members (or potential team members) as possible. Why? First, it helps you "dream big" in reframing and clarifying the goal to create a compelling vision of the project's end result and its value to the organization. Second, it begins the building of a shared passion about the project that will drive the team's desire to get the job done in exceptional fashion.

As you work to articulate the project goal, try to boil it down to its essence and then run this by team members. Ask if it makes sense. Ask if they have better ways to shape the goal statement. Ask their take on the problem this project will fix or the opportunity this project will seize. You want to draw widely to yield the most compelling and useful project definition you can. At the same time, you want to begin building a burning desire in people to want to be a part of your project team (even if they are assigned to the team by no choice of their own). You want and need clear vision and passion from your team about the project goal.

Setting the project goal requires a multichannel, team-wide dialogue that creates clarity and passion for the project team.

The Criteria to Use—"Power Goals"

As you work to establish the project goal in end user outcome terms, you will find it very helpful to state the goal in terms of five important elements. These characteristics are captured in the term POWER, an acronym for the aspects of a goal that are likely to provide focus and create commitment for the project. POWER goals are *pinpointed*, *owned*, *well defined*, *energizing*, and *resource framed*.

Pinpointed. Your goal should be so pinpointed, so specific, and so clear that anybody with some basic knowledge of the project area can read it, understand it, and know what you are trying to accomplish. Can it pass the "you've only got one minute to explain the project to a new team member" test? Could you drop dead tomorrow (of course, we do not recommend that you test it this way) and somebody else pick up the goal statement and know exactly the project's purpose? It should be that clearly framed.

For example, a non-pinpointed goal might be stated:

We need a new marketing piece.

But for what product, by whom, at what cost? To pinpoint this goal, we might say:

We need a new marketing brochure for product X within three months at a cost of less than $15,000.

This second statement makes much clearer what needs to be accomplished, with much less chance of confusion by the end user or the team.

<u>O</u>**wned.** For a goal to be effective, ownership must be created and based on understanding and buy-in from all parties. The end user, be it a customer, upper management, or a peer in your organization, must agree that the project goal is desirable. Stated differently, the project leader and the project's "customer" must agree that the end result should solve the problem or respond to the need that led to the initiation of the project. The more that people agree upon and own the goal up front, the easier it will be to develop a viable plan for the project. This solid ownership will make it easier to respond to changes that may require modifying the goal as the project unfolds. Ownership is based on sharing information, and it builds commitment and passion for the project.

Sometimes reaching agreement and ownership can be difficult. It may take extensive dialogue to help all parties understand each other. And it usually helps if you, the project leader, can focus on understanding what the end user really needs. Those needs should be the ultimate focus for defining the agreed-upon aspect of the goal. By identifying and focusing on these needs, you build into the goal a sense of meaning and significance for the project. And passion, energy, and commitment flow from the ownership-building process.

<u>W</u>**ell defined.** To manage a project to successful completion, you must create a well-defined description of what successful completion will look like. You must be able to *measure* the goal to know the real outcome of the project. What will be different and how will we know it is different? Ineffective project leaders often wrongly say that some project goals cannot be measured. But every goal can be measured; it's just that some goals can be measured more easily than others can. In fact, developing clear measuring standards for the more ambiguous and fuzzy kinds of goals is where you should spend the most time. The risk of confusion is too great in these situations for you to fail to spend time creating useful measures. Without well-defined goals, members of your team cannot acquire any sense of direction, and they wind up like the archer shooting at the wrong target or no target at all. Project participants need to work on measurable activities, even if the measures are crude, in order to know what to do. And you need a well-defined goal if you are to try to reach it.

*Every goal can be well defined with measures; it's just that
some goals can be defined more easily than others.*

For example, Ken Blanchard, co-author of *The One Minute Manager*, describes how a large bank wanted to create an image of friendliness, but nobody knew how to measure friendliness. Top management felt that bank personnel were not friendly, and a survey of customers confirmed this impression. The consultants called in to work with the bank decided, after much discussion with bank personnel, to measure friendliness in a unique way. They would count the number of comments between customers and bank personnel unrelated to work—comments about the weather, about how somebody was dressed, or about how cousin Johnny was feeling these days. The consultants found that very few of the comments between bank personnel and their customers were of this non-task-related variety (about one comment per customer interaction).

The goal established for the "friendliness project" was to increase the number of non-task-related comments per customer interaction from one to four. All bank personnel got involved. They talked about the goal with the consultants, they discussed examples of what to say, and they worked at it. After five weeks of observing, the consultants determined that the number of non-task-related comments per interaction had risen to four. A follow-up customer survey revealed that their perception of the bank's friendliness had gone up dramatically. Now this is not a particularly brilliant measure of friendliness, but it worked because it helped quantify what people should do. It gave people a target they could aim at. They could also measure their own progress. Having clear measuring standards is a vital part of the process of setting effective goals. Such standards as quantity, quality, time, and cost are the most useful to work with in establishing measurable standards.

Energizing.   Project goals must be energizing, and this energy comes from a feeling that the goal is realistic and doable, yet challenging. All too often managers set goals that are impossible to achieve, given the resources, knowledge, and time available. And project leaders who allow this to happen set up themselves and their teams for frustration that saps energy. This does not mean that goals should be easy to achieve. They can and should be challenging in order to build energy, but if they are unrealistic, they will instead diminish energy. How many times have you been assigned a project and a deadline before the goal is clarified, only to find out that the project cannot possibly be completed on time? When you and your team realize the impossibility of the situation, everyone tends to give up before the race even begins.

One of the benefits you derive from dialogue in the goal-setting process is determining whether you are talking about a goal that is realistic, given your resources. You have to question this assumption explicitly. Don't just say, "Sure, we can get that done." Discuss resources, budgets, personnel, and timing to determine how realistic the goal is. Making it realistic may mean adjusting the goal, the deadline, or the resources, but realism is critical for the energy that leads to success.

Energy that comes from the project itself also means that even though the project is unique and different from your past experience, it should not be totally alien to project personnel. If it is, you are asking for trouble. In this case you will need to set aside time for research and learning, or perhaps engage consultants or hire new project members or even delay the project. You should not get trapped into doing things you know too little about, unless you want to fail.

But by the same token, you should not just take on projects that are a snap. Energy comes from taking on goals that are a challenge and that make a difference in your organization. Passion is a must, and it comes from the joy of tackling a challenge that is a stretch, but not a stretch to the breaking point of your and your team's will and ability.

Resource framed. Finally, you need a goal that is resource framed. How much time and budget do you have to accomplish the project? Is there any flexibility in the deadline? Is there any flexibility in the resources available for the project? This goes back to looking at what is attainable. You want to set a deadline that is reasonable, given the resources available and the amount of knowledge and experience you have with this type of project. In addition, you want everyone involved in the team to clearly know the resource constraints and deadline so they can act in an empowered fashion to help get the job done on time, within budget, and with high quality. Clarity about resources is critical to project success.

An Example of a Really Important Goal

Consider, for example, the project that God gave to Noah. God's voice boomed, "Build an ark of gopher wood, 300 cubits long, 50 cubits wide, and 30 cubits high. And do it in seven months, when I will destroy the earth by flood. Take a male and female of every animal; we are starting over." Pretty important goal, right? If Noah had failed, the entire human race would be wiped out; Noah had to develop a POWER goal and an effective plan for the sake of all people on the earth.

So, let's see. Was the goal **P**inpointed? Yes, it was clear that Noah had to build an ark. **O**wned and agreed-upon? Who can argue with God? Noah believed God was telling the truth about the coming flood; hence he accepted the fact that he needed to accomplish the goal. **W**ell defined? Not too clear on the animals but clear on the dimensions of the ark. **E**nergizing, based on a feeling the goal was realistic? Yes, Noah was a fisherman who knew about boats; he knew it was possible to build this ark. **R**esource framed? Yes and no. Rains were to begin in seven months; costs not clarified. So we can imagine some discussion between Noah and God about the project planning—Noah questioning God on size, type of wood, animals to be excluded/included, why the flood; and God explaining and refining the goal until Noah was completely clear about it. Perhaps you have similar discussions with your supervisors. The question to ask is, does your project have a POWER goal? If not, keep working at it until your project goal meets the POWER criteria.

Why not take a minute now to write down the goal for one of your projects. Then check it against the POWER criteria. Is your project goal a POWER goal: Is it pinpointed, owned, well defined, energizing, and resource framed?

The importance of spending sufficient time and energy on the goal-setting process cannot be overemphasized. To paraphrase what winning project team leaders have told us: Goal setting takes significant time and energy, but you can't reach the finish line and get the checkered flag without clear and compelling goals! Effective goal setting is crucial for your projects because it provides a common vision that gives members of the team a sense of ownership. Clear goals build excitement and passion. They keep the team members focused through to the project's completion.

Project goal not a POWER goal? You are in the slow lane, heading for disappointment and away from the checkered flag that goes to a winning project team!

Before we leave this first rule of effective project leadership, let us again emphasize that a POWER goal needs to become a common vision for every member of the team as well as for the end user. It is your job to keep everyone's eyes focused on that target until it is fully achieved. You cannot let the flame of passion burn out before the job is done if you want that checkered flag!

How can you ensure that people keep their eyes on the goal? First, make certain that the goal is in writing and is distributed to everybody on your team. Second, constantly remind people what the goal is. One of the primary responsibilities of a project leader is to keep the overall vision of the goal squarely in front of people. Third, be sure that project team members always know what they are trying to accomplish for the person or group who will ultimately use their product. Doing this improves communication, reduces tension, empowers team members to contribute and monitor their efforts relative to the goal. Bottom line, it helps ensure that your project will be completed on time, within budget, and with high quality. Everyone will be cheering when you and your team cross the finish line of the race to a waving checkered flag!

Summary

Rule One:
Clarify the Project Goal

1. Project success begins with defining the end result, the goal: create it, reframe it, boil it down, share it.

2. Effective project leaders keep their eyes on the goal and make sure that everybody else on the team (including the end user) does too.

3. Effective project leaders develop a POWER goal, involving lots of people so that the goal is clear and compelling.

4. Creating a common and compelling vision for the project empowers team members to use their skills, experience, and motivation to help get the job done on time, within budget, and with high quality.

5. Goal setting is a must-do first step in building the vehicle that will power you to the checkered flag. Without the "**G**" in your **GOCART-S**, failure is right around the first curve on the race track.

Goal clarified
   O
     C
       A
         R
           T
             S

Rule Two:
Use Objectives to Define Responsibilities

If individuals are to be empowered to get the project done, they need clear objectives linked to the overall project goal.

Once you and your team have gone through the goal-setting process and have a clear idea of where the project as a whole needs to go, you are ready to add more detail to your plan. The goal guides the team as a whole, but you cannot operate simply with a goal. Noah, for example, needed more detail than just the command "Build an ark." So does your project team. You must add the **"O"** to **GOCART-S** and establish **O**bjectives that can guide and focus each team member's efforts.

Objectives are guiding principles that direct the efforts of team members in their contribution to the project's goal. You need one or more objectives for each person involved. Objectives serve to clarify what the person must accomplish but also to create the passion each person will need to get the job done. In addition, team members need to know how everyone's work ties together to accomplish the project goal. This knowledge helps team members manage the interfaces that pull people together to achieve the common project goal.

Specifying objectives helps you identify who needs to be on the team (i.e., what skill mix is required). Objectives break down the goal into a set of specific tasks. They tell each person what to do, when to do it, and how to measure progress. In essence, the project objectives are subgoals of the overall project goal. Accomplishment of all the objectives in an integrated fashion leads to accomplishment of the overall project goal. The process of defining objectives is a first step in what is often called the *Work Breakdown Structure* (see Figure 2.1).

If, for example, your project is to install a new computer system so that people have faster access to performance data, you might assign one person the objective of preparing the site for the computer. Another person might take the objective of ordering the computer and delivering it to the installation site. A third person might be responsible for setting up the computer, and a fourth person might have the job of debugging the computer to make sure it operates as intended. Once these objectives are reached, your project team will have completed the goal of installing a new computer system that works on the user's premises.

In essence, objectives can be viewed as "little" goals with a more narrow scope than the project goal and also linked to the project goal. Just as with the project goal, a back-and-forth dialogue between the project leader and the team members who will complete the objectives ensures that well-defined objectives are established. It is also a good idea to apply the POWER criteria to each objective. An effective objective must be pinpointed, owned, well defined, energizing, and resource framed. Otherwise, objectives cannot effectively guide the behavior of project team members.

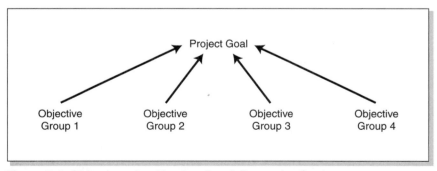

Figure 2.1 Objectives Are Used to Break Down the Goal

A key impact of POWER objectives is that they establish guidelines within which team members have both the autonomy and responsibility to contribute. POWER objectives are critical for creating an empowered project team. By connecting objectives with specific team members and using a dialogue around the POWER criteria, you create the clarity and passion that is needed to tap the experience, knowledge, and motivation that reside within each team member—both individually and collectively as a team.

> *Ownership leads team members to take responsibility*
> *and feel a passion and commitment to accomplish*
> *their objectives that support the project goal.*

Just as you did with the project goal, put the project objectives in writing and literally hang them on the wall. That way, they constantly remind the team and focus each individual to accomplish what is needed to earn the checkered flag for the project. One company we worked with made a companywide commitment to zero defects. Everyone signed a pledge to contribute to that goal and each of these signed statements was displayed on the lobby walls of the corporate offices. The company eventually guaranteed complete accuracy in its shipment to all customers, and they routinely come very close to their goal of perfection.

What about Noah and the ark? What are some of the objectives that Noah might have established with the team members to achieve the primary project goal? Several possibilities are shown in Figure 2.2. Noah took the overall goal of building an ark and then began to specify the responsibilities of the different functional groups that needed to contribute to its completion.

Research on peak-performing individuals and groups confirms that clarity of objectives plus passion about the objectives are essential for effective project performance. Team members must know where they are headed and they must be committed to getting there; otherwise, the race is already lost. This sense of direction and buy-in substantially increases the chances of getting to the project finish line on time, within budget, and with high quality.

**Noah's Ark Project
(Sample Objectives)**

Objectives for woodcutters:
Cut 600 pieces of gopher wood, each 10 feet long by 1 foot wide by 3 inches thick. Have this done in two months.

Objectives for carpenters:
Take the 600 pieces of gopher wood and fit them together into an ark 300 cubits long, 50 cubits wide, and 30 cubits high. Do this in three months.

Objectives for the animal handlers:
Find the best-looking and strongest male and female of each species of animal. No rejects, please. Get them here in two months.

Figure 2.2 POWER Objectives for the Noah's Ark Project

Problems in Setting Objectives

As with project goal setting, many people have difficulty in setting project objectives. Objectives should be designed so that their accomplishment logically leads to achievement of the project goal. But, as you know, there are times when it just does not work out that way. Sometimes things do not go according to plan. Why does this occur and what can you do about it?

Focusing Too Narrowly.   Unfortunately, objectives can sometimes become blinders that restrict an individual's vision of other people's objectives and the project goal. Think about what happens when people start to work on *their* objectives. The objectives become their focus day in and day out, making it easy for them to lose sight of the end result: the project goal. Also, one person can easily lose sight of the objectives of the other team members working on the project. People readily go off on a tangent and forget to inform others of what they are doing. As a result, they may accomplish their objectives in ways that make it more difficult for other team members to accomplish their objectives, thus inhibiting overall goal accomplishment.

People lost in the detail of their objectives often lose sight of the big picture—the project goal. Manufacturing builds a product that can't be marketed cost effectively. Marketing promises customized products when operations are based on a mass production system. The key to avoiding too narrow a focus is to keep the project goal out in the open. To combat the tendency to focus too narrowly, you as project leader must constantly remind team members of the project goal.

Ensure that everyone keeps the project goal in direct sight, even while pursuing particular objectives.

Using Reward Systems That Inhibit Teamwork. Reward systems in many organizations tend to push project team members apart. Instead of fostering cooperation to achieve the project goal, they create competitiveness as team members work on their own individual objectives. Typically, reward systems focus too much attention on the accomplishment of objectives for each functional group and not enough on the accomplishment of the project goal.

A good example of this breakdown occurred at a naval air station that had four squadrons responsible for the maintenance of planes. The stated goal was to have 95 percent of all planes ready to go at any time. Actual readiness was running around 85 percent. The new commanding officer decided he would reassert this goal of 95 percent and back it up with a reward system. Each month, he would reward the squadron having the highest percentage of plane readiness with, for example, a 24-hour pass or public recognition of a job well done. What happened?

The members of one squadron decided that the secret to success was to have a well-stocked parts inventory. Then if a plane came in with a broken radar part, they could simply take that part out and put in a replacement and the plane would be ready to go again. They also realized that if they could increase their parts inventory while decreasing the parts inventory for the other squadrons, they would be well on the way to winning this competition. The obvious solution? Steal parts! This may sound ridiculous, but it is a true story.

One of the squadrons began to engage in midnight requisitions to steal parts from the other squadrons. The other squadrons figured out what was going on and decided to retaliate. Soon all four squadrons were stealing from each other. Every squadron put guards on duty 24 hours a day, 7 days a week to protect inventories. Meanwhile, the percentage of planes ready to go was going downhill fast.

The problem wasn't the people or the lack of a clear goal; it was the reward system. People knew the overall goal but felt that their own squadron's objectives were more important, especially since these objectives were what was to be rewarded. A simple change in the reward system solved the problem. After the change, any and all squadrons that achieved the goal of 95 percent readiness for the month would get the reward. What happened? First, the stealing stopped. The squadrons started sharing parts to help one another out. The readiness percentage quickly rose to 90 percent and began pushing toward 95 percent—all because the reward system was changed to support the accomplishment of both the objectives and the project goal.

As a project leader, you can't set the objectives and then forget about them. An ancient proverb captures this well: "People do not do what the leader expects, but what the leader inspects and rewards." It is foolish to expect a result when you are not rewarding that result but are instead rewarding something else. If you want people to cooperate on a project and to keep the overall goal in mind, you will have to reward their cooperative efforts toward accomplishing the project goal.

Reward efforts that support the overall project goal,
not just the objectives of individual team members.

Responsibility but Not Enough Authority. Another significant problem for project leaders is that they are often responsible for results but lack authority to get the job done. Think about the typical setup of a project. Suppose the new company computer will affect four departments: information systems, accounting, fulfillment, and customer relations. Within each department, people report to a department manager. Several of these people also report to the project leader in charge of the new computer system changeover. Thus, people have two bosses—their department manager and the project manager. Let's say the project accounts for half their responsibilities, departmental matters the other half. But who evaluates these people at the end of the year? The project manager? No. The department manager. So if there is any conflict in what the two managers tell an employee to do, what will the person do? Ignore or put off the project manager. It's only logical and makes good sense to the individual team members.

To succeed as a project leader in this context, you must influence people in different functional groups to cooperate and to coordinate efforts so that no team member is asked to do two things at the same time. You need to have significant input into the evaluation of the team members, working in conjunction with each person's department manager. When team members know that both managers will be engaged in evaluating their performance, they are more motivated to do what both managers say.

Let's go one step further, though, and ask how we can get the information systems, accounting, fulfillment, and customer relations managers to cooperate with the project manager. In many cases, department managers have no real accountability for a project. But in companies where the project manager approach works best, department managers are held partly responsible for the success of the project. The division manager evaluates department managers not only in terms of department activities but also in terms of how well the project is succeeding. The department managers then have a reason to cooperate and work with the project leader to help get the job done. Each individual department manager has a stake in the project and knows that rewards and evaluations depend on project success. The department managers focus not only on the project objectives involving their department but also on the overall success of the project. The department managers will more readily cooperate and coordinate with one another and with the project leader.

Now, it's a good guess that your organization may not have this kind of formalized project accountability for department managers. And if it does not, you can't afford to just throw up your hands. Instead, use the informal organization. Go outside the hierarchy to develop a relationship with each of the department managers and draw them into the project. Get them on your side and make them understand how you are going to help them. In other words, develop a relationship with the department managers. Help them develop a stake in the project's success. And by all means, see how you can help them in their department and thank them for helping you with the project.

Use the informal organization to augment your influence and achieve project success.

For example, consider the situation of a marketing analyst for a large oil company. To complete projects, the analyst had to get information from salespeople in the field, but she had no authority over them. To go through the organizational channels up several levels, across, and then down several levels to ask a sales rep to provide information would take months. And the sales reps had no stake in the project. So the analyst worked on relationships with the salespeople. In fact, she went out and rode the territory with the sales reps, talked with them, and got to know them. Then, when she called to ask for information, it was not just the marketing analyst calling; it was someone they knew. Even though the system may not support you by coordinating the objectives of different departments, you can ensure that those objectives tie in to the project goal by working through the informal organization to build dependable relationships. These relationships will prove invaluable in getting your project to the finish line successfully.

Summary

Rule Two:
Use Objectives to Define Responsibilities

1. Define POWER objectives through dialogue with team members; break down the project goal into specific responsibilities for each team member.

2. Objectives identify who should be on a project team and also establish ownership for key elements of the project plan.

3. Keep people from focusing *only* on their objectives and thus losing sight of the overall project goal, as well as how their work links to the work of others!

4. Establish rewards that are linked to overall project success, as well as to success on the objectives.

5. Be certain that responsibility for each project objective carries corresponding authority.

6. Use objectives to build clarity and passion about each team member's responsibilities on the project.

Goal clarified
  Objectives and responsibilities defined
    C
      A
        R
          T
            S

Rule Three:
Establish Checkpoints, Activities, Relationships, and Time Estimates

Involve all team members in planning the race so you have an excellent route that is clear to everyone.

The **G** and **O** (for **G**oals and **O**bjectives) establish where your project is going and how each team member will contribute to the end result. But without a planned route you can easily wind up driving in circles, making no progress. To get to the finish line, you need a well-designed **CART**. You and your team must define, initiate, and revise as necessary **C**heckpoints, **A**ctivities, **R**elationships among the activities, and **T**ime (cost and other resource) estimates.

Without a **CART**—an action plan—you will not know if you are making progress toward the objectives and final goal. Also, how will you know when to slow down or speed up? How will you know how much time and money you will need or how much you have used? You must add further detail to your plan by assembling the vehicle that will take you to the finish line. And there is no express lane for this work. You and your team must roll up your sleeves, think about and analyze what needs to be done to power your engine, and tune the result as precisely as you can. These steps continue the Work Breakdown Structure we began in Rule Two.

Checkpoints are like mile markers on a route to let drivers know they are headed in the right direction. They serve as visible reminders of progress. Without them, you may not even realize that your project has strayed way off track. Without them, team members have little way of coordinating their work to accomplish the overall goal. Checkpoints, when set and shared, galvanize team members with energy and responsibility. Individuals will not want to let down their team members, the project as a whole, or themselves.

Checkpoints serve as visible reminders of progress.

There are both long-term and short-term checkpoints.

The long-term checkpoints are called *milestones*. They measure actual versus planned progress on projects and serve as visible and tangible measures of movement toward project completion. Milestones mark the completion of significant events and tell you whether your project is on schedule, behind schedule, or ahead of schedule.

If, for example, you are in a cross-country race from Atlanta to Los Angeles, some of the major milestones might be Birmingham, Dallas, and Phoenix. Reaching these cities at the designated times would indicate that you are on course for your final destination and that you are on schedule. Missing them would mean that you are off track and need to make adjustments. For example, if you found yourself in Chicago on your trip to Los Angeles, you would know you had made a wrong turn. Clearly, you would like to have known this before you got so far off track. To avoid such big mistakes, you need short-term checkpoints.

Short-term checkpoints are called *events*. They are similar to milestones, but they occur more frequently, and thus there are more of them. Several events usually lead up to a particular milestone. Events provide feedback on a more regular, ongoing basis. They are useful at the operational level, whereas milestones provide more of an overview that is useful at a managerial level.

For example, on your race from Atlanta to Los Angeles, some of the events might be getting onto Interstate 20 heading west out of Atlanta or reaching Meridian, Mississippi, a small town between Birmingham and Dallas. Events simply add further detail to the project course and quickly tell you if you are headed down the wrong road. Now, if in Atlanta you go east on I-20, you will know right away that you made a mistake and can correct it.

Checkpoints mark a specific instance in time, the accomplishment of something. **Activities** are the tasks that carry you from one event to the next, then to your milestones, and eventually to achieving project objectives and the overall project goal. Activities are the tasks that must be completed in order to complete the project. In defining a project, you want to identify activities as precisely and in as much detail as possible. Don't overlook any activity necessary to complete the project, no matter how small. On your trip to Los Angeles, for example, failure to check your oil at a gas station stop could halt your entire project if the engine burns up because of low oil.

As Figure 3.1 illustrates, goals, objectives, checkpoints, and activities are highly interrelated and are crucial in any project journey. Working with your team to think through the checkpoints and events and begin-

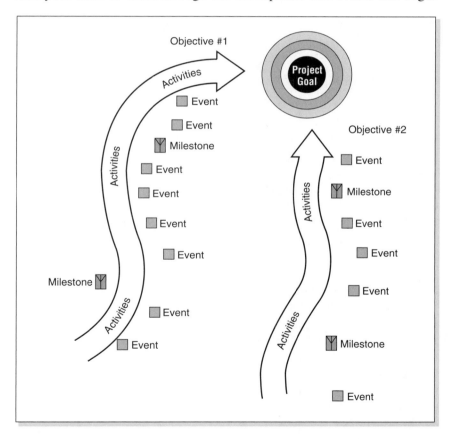

Figure 3.1 Establish Checkpoints, Activities, and Relationships That Lead to the Objectives and Goal

ning to list activities will typically generate additional events and milestones that you did not think of at first. Creating this level of detail is another step in the Work Breakdown Structure process.

But remember to keep in mind the larger perspective of the goal and objectives as you and your team become increasingly more precise in looking at the milestones, the events, and the required activities. You need to go from an overall picture down to the individual details. What you are doing is working backward from the goal of the project to the first step that you have to take to get to that goal. What is the first turn you take on your race to Los Angeles? Which way do you turn out of your driveway?

By doing this work as a team you create a synergy that will pay huge dividends later in the project management phase. This dialogue among team members builds a better plan for the project that is understood by all, and the effort also creates an energy that comes from involvement and open sharing of responsibility for the activities.

Examining the Noah's Ark Project

Let's take another look at Noah's project of building and stocking the ark. What were some of the milestones, events, and activities?

Consider the carpenter's objective of building the ark according to specifications. This objective involves a complex process. Milestones and events add detail to the objective; they break it down into more manageable pieces. If Noah and the carpenters had had only the objective of completing the ark, all the thousands of additional things that were needed might never have been done, and, as a result, the ark might never have been completed.

How did Noah's establishment of milestones and events help Noah define his route and then monitor progress? Sample milestones might have been a completed layout of the ark, the skeleton of the ark built, and a male and female of each species in the waiting pen. Each milestone marked a major event. By combining these with time estimates for the activities, Noah could know whether he was ahead of schedule, behind schedule, or on schedule. Had he known only that he needed to reach a milestone in a month, he might not have had enough feedback to guide his direction and enable him to monitor his progress. He needed more specific direction.

Events provided that detail. Some of the events along the path to completing the ark's skeleton were putting the vertical supports on each side in place, nailing on the side supports, and connecting the two sides. Noah could identify several events in the process of reaching the milestone of a completed skeleton, and those events gave him more detail. Listing the events also helped him define the actions he had to complete in building the ark. When he finished determining the events and activities, he had the beginnings of a route. Adding time estimates, he could know one week into this seven-month project that he needed to have the side layout completed. He knew that if he did not have this part of the layout, he was behind schedule. If he did have the layout, he was on schedule. As he defined the first step, the second step, and the third, he made the project more manageable. This is one of the primary advantages of having checkpoints and activities. They help to define exactly what you should be doing to get a project done. An activity is more manageable than a project. Figure 3.2 summarizes part of the Work Breakdown Structure for one objective in the ark project—putting the ark together. It details the milestones, events, and activities breakdown for this objective.

Sample Objective for Noah's Ark Project:
Carpenters Put Ark Together

Milestones	Events	Activities
A. One side of ark completed	1. Side supports built 2. Side slats installed 3. Railing built and mounted 4. Bottom support beam added	a. Build vertical supports b. Build horizontal supports c. Nail on slats d. Paint leak filler on slats e. Build and mount railing f. Cut ramp opening g. Nail bottom support beam
B. Second side of ark completed	(Similar to above)	

Figure 3.2 Breaking Down an Objective into Milestones, Events, and Activities

Monitoring as Motivation

Milestones and events also give you and your team a useful way to monitor progress on the project. People can continually check to determine if the project is on schedule. But perhaps the most valuable result that comes from having milestones, events, and activities is that they help to motivate and guide individual responsibility on the project. They are an integral part of empowering people to get the job done.

Checkpoints are an essential form of feedback that keeps project team members committed, energized, motivated, and empowered for success. They help team members monitor themselves and teammates so that together they keep the project on schedule, within budget, and up to high-quality standards. Feedback has been called "the breakfast of champions." People thrive on it. Information that is related to goals and objectives is essential for empowerment.

By giving your team members milestones and events, you draw up a map for them so they can measure their location precisely. Remember the "W" (for well defined) in POWER goals and objectives? Clear definition and measurement continue to be critical throughout the entire planning process.

Without a detailed map, people may stray from the road and not achieve their particular objective, let alone the overall project goal. By guiding the team to develop a well-conceived set of milestones and events, you provide them with a map to track their own progress and allow them to become and remain excited about the project. They know what the project goal is—you've reminded them of it. They know what their objectives are—you've clarified them for each team member. The checkpoints and activities provide points on the map that each individual can use as a tracking system to check his or her progress. Each person knows that the objective is to reach Dallas by Tuesday afternoon. If they pass Marshall, Texas, at noon, they know that they are on schedule. People tend to feel excited when they know they are on track and making progress.

In addition, milestones and events provide the map coordinates that help you figure out the best way to get back on track when your project does get lost. They help you engage in contingency planning when things fall behind schedule. They also make it less likely you will be too far off course, thus making it easier to get back on track. Indeed, when the checkpoints are clear to all team members, they will help each other stay on course or get back on course in many cases with little or no involvement from the project leader: a great time saver for you, indeed.

> *Milestones and events motivate team members to successfully*
> *complete the project and to take the checkered flag!*

Milestones and events also give you and the team opportunities to celebrate meaningful progress and to recognize people's contributions. All too often, project managers overlook these opportunities. By knowing precisely what the schedule is and by being aware of it as people meet their checkpoints, you can give them a pat on the back. This simple act does wonders in terms of keeping people energized and excited about the project. You don't want to be like the bowling team captain who, when a teammate knocks down seven of the ten pins on the first ball, yells, "You missed three." Effective project managers use this opportunity to say, "Fantastic. You knocked down seven. The 3, 5, and 7 pins are left. Good luck on the second ball." You are monitoring progress. You are giving feedback to people. You are recognizing people's performance levels— praising them for their contributions or solving problems with them when they're behind schedule or not meeting expectations.

All of these opportunities for positive feedback are possible with clear checkpoints and clear assignments for the activities that lead to the checkpoints. The passion for the project goal can now be transferred to the level of specific actions that lead to goal accomplishment.

Determining Relationships Among the Activities

With a well-thought-out list of the activities that make up a project, you and your team are ready for the important step of determining the **Relationships** among the activities. Here the action plan becomes even more concrete and begins to truly look like a road map for success. The essential point is to recognize that certain activities may need to be performed before others can be performed, but some activities can be performed simultaneously. From this analysis comes a clear coordinated plan for the team. For example, on the ark, Noah's team had to build the frame before adding the side slats, but they could build the vertical supports at the same time as the horizontal supports.

The questions you and your team need to answer are:

- What is the necessary order in which the activities must be done?
- What is the logical flow of activities?
- What do technological requirements and resource availability dictate about the flow of activities?

You will often find that there is more than one way to complete the project. Determining the possible relationships among activities will help you identify efficient ways to get the job done and plan for alternatives to cope with unexpected contingencies.

There is always more than one way to do the job;
take enough time to consider the options.

Getting the job done seldom depends on doing things in one right way. Perhaps two activities can be done in parallel rather than in tandem. Perhaps an activity one group was going to do can be done by another group. Try to anticipate the unexpected and consider ways to deal with it.

It is at this point that you address the "What if?" and "What could go wrong?" questions. What if this activity does not work out the way you think it will? What are some options if you encounter difficulties? Here you are engaged in contingency planning, a very important element in project planning.

Contingency planning helps you and your team focus on the alternatives in a creative fashion. You can brainstorm different ways to get a task completed, that is, different sequences of activities. You can focus on what to do when things do not go according to plan by addressing alternative sequencing options for the activities that lead to accomplishing the objective (more on contingency planning to come with Rule Four). Just be sure not to lose sight of your goal during this creative step in the process. But at the same time, allow the team to build energy through creatively addressing the question of relationships among activities.

Estimating Time, Cost, and Other Resources

The final element in completing the Work Breakdown Structure is to determine *accurate* estimates of the amount of **Time** (plus cost and other resources) each activity will require. Such estimates allow you to plan the project more completely. Who needs to be involved in building the sides of Noah's ark? How long will it take? What will it cost?

Unfortunately, these decisions have to be made with limited information. Usually, you do not know exactly how long a particular activity will take. You do not know precisely what resources will be needed, or how much they will cost: each project is unique. The process of estimating time and other resource requirements is especially challenging because you cannot accurately predict the future and because things are likely to change once you implement the plan. But with clearly defined activities, you can better identify the time, cost, and other resources needed to complete each activity. Even if it is difficult to make accurate estimates, it is still worth the effort to do as good a job as possible and then refine estimates later as necessary.

One estimation strategy for achieving accuracy when dealing with uncertain or unfamiliar activities actually requires coming up with three estimates. This process works equally well for both time and cost estimates. Let us focus on time to illustrate the three estimates. The first estimate is an optimistic one: for example, the shortest possible time if everything falls into place in completing the activity. The second estimate is a pessimistic one: the time it will take if many things go wrong and you run into many difficulties. The third estimate is the most likely time: the time with the normal array of pluses and minuses. Such careful thinking helps you to further assess "what could go wrong" and what is really involved in completing an activity.

In making these three time estimates, consult with team members who have relevant experience about how long an activity will take. This information will help you refine your estimates. As a side benefit, involving people in the estimation process builds their commitment to the eventual time estimate. It encourages the attitude, "We told Noah we could find a male and female kangaroo in two days, and, by God, we'll do it!" Recognizing that all three numbers will still be estimates, you can calculate a weighted average to get a better idea of how long the activity will take. The equation for this calculation is shown in Figure 3.3, where by custom the "most likely" estimate is weighted four times as likely to occur as either the "optimistic" or "pessimistic" estimates.

The time an activity will consume will probably fall somewhere between the pessimistic and the optimistic times, and a precise estimate for the activity would be the expected time that comes out of the equation in Figure 3.3. This kind of calculation is not needed for every activity in a

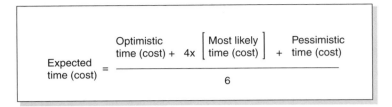

Figure 3.3 Equation for Time (Cost) Estimates

project, but it is useful for critical activities with which you have little experience. Even if you do not go through the math, using this thought process will lead to more accurate time (and cost) estimates for project activities.

Remember that in making time and cost estimates for activities, it is crucial to think through the resources needed to complete each activity. By identifying the people, equipment, and other resource needs, it becomes easier to build accurate time and cost estimates.

As a general principle, however, it is always advisable to build some slack (extra resources, costs, and time) into your estimates. No one can predict the future with crystal ball certainty. Despite our best efforts at estimating, we almost always leave something out of the calculation or some unforeseen and unanticipated activity takes place. Slack is the grease that effective project leaders use to maneuver the project back on track. But by the same token, it is not advisable to build in unnecessary slack. Accurate estimates are the desired result of the estimating process. Hitting a time target within plus or minus a small amount is far better for the overall project success than coming in way under an unrealistically high (heavy slack) estimate.

The key is to avoid wild guesses or rough estimates. Invest the necessary energy to come up with as accurate an estimate of time, cost, and other resources needs as possible for each activity. Otherwise, your **GOCART** is likely to go way off track.

> *Accurate estimates are what is desired,*
> *not loose, self-serving estimates.*

Even then, it is important to recognize that these times (or costs) are estimates. Only after you have completed an activity will you really know how long it takes or how many other resources are needed. If you have done a similar project before, you may have a much better idea of how long it will take to complete an activity. But even then, the uniqueness of each project dictates that the resource figures you use are still

Sample Objective for Noah's Ark Project: Carpenters Put Ark Together

Milestones	Events	Activities	What Activities Must Precede?	Time Estimate	Who Does It?	Cost (in Talents)
A. One side of ark completed	1. Side supports built	a. Build vertical supports		14 days	Noah's son Shem	250
	2. Side slats installed	b. Build horizontal supports		10 days	Noah's son Ham	200
	3. Railing built and mounted	c. Nail on slats	a, b	14 days	Shem and Ham	75
	4. Bottom support beam added	d. Paint leak filler on slats	c	7 days	Noah's son Japheth	28
		e. Build and mount railing	a, b	2 days	Shem	15
		f. Cut ramp opening	d, e	1 day	Shem	5
		g. Nail bottom support beam	d	4 days	Ham and Japheth	12

Figure 3.4 The Work Breakdown Structure for One Objective in the Noah's Ark Project

estimates. Figure 3.4 shows the time estimates, the activity relationships, and the division of responsibility for each activity on one part of the Noah's Ark project.

Final Thoughts on Building a CART

In this third rule, we have presented a number of ideas for building detail into your project plans. You may be thinking, "I'm not sure I have the time to do such extensive planning." You may also be wondering, "Can you overplan a project?" Well, the answer is, "Yes, but most likely you don't need to worry about that as of now." If you keep talking and talking and talking with your team about the elements of your **CART**, you can bleed off the energy needed to get moving with the project. But more commonly, people fall prey to the activity trap of jumping to action with no clear idea of where they are going. The art of project planning is to build consensus around a well-designed plan without dragging down the initial enthusiasm for the project.

Your ability to sense a growing consensus is the key. Pay attention to the point when "What if?" and "What could go wrong?" and "What are some alternatives?" questions begin to subside. Also, pay attention to when most team members begin to nod their heads in agreement. These signals tell you the plan is coming together, at least for now. Does it mean the plan will never change? No. But it does mean you now have a workable plan that can focus and stoke the energy of the team members.

Finally, to put some perspective into your thinking, keep in mind how hard it has been to keep people motivated and working to complete a project that was following a poor or nonexistent plan. Maybe, just maybe, your time would be well spent to develop a workable plan from the start. We certainly think so. Put another way, most project leaders have a long way to go before they have to worry about overplanning a project!

Summary

Rule Three:
Establish Checkpoints, Activities, Relationships, and Time Estimates

1. Develop a **CART** for your project by defining **Checkpoints** to mark your progress, **Activities** to get the project done, **Relationships** to clarify the flow of activities, and **Time** (cost and other resource) estimates to complete each activity.

2. In breaking down the elements of a project, work backward from the goal to the very first step that must be taken to accomplish that goal.

3. People work best when they know their responsibilities and have ways to track their progress. Establish milestones, events, and assigned activities to help team members monitor project progress and motivate themselves.

4. Be creative and thorough as relationships among the project activities are considered. Be sure to include "What if?" and "What could go wrong?" scenarios to create better contingency plans.

5. Create accurate estimates of the time and cost necessary to complete each activity of a project.

6. Don't overplan the project, but also, don't underestimate the power of a clear plan and consensus among team members!

7. Your **GOCART** is now complete and ready for the race:

Goal clarified
  Objectives and responsibilities defined
    Checkpoints established
      Activities established
        Relationships established
          Time (cost) estimates set

Rule Four: Supercharge the Plan with a Picture

A picture is worth a thousand words.

So far your planning efforts have been rewarded with a **GOCART** plan that is well designed and has energized your team to get the job done. But there is one more important step in the planning process that will allow you to work more quickly and with higher quality, especially when you encounter surprises to the plan. You can now use pictures and related software to Supercharge the plan.

Unfortunately, the many project leaders who fail to use these powerful tools relegate themselves to the category of project leaders who lose races. Let's make you a winner! By using project plan pictures, you achieve seven advantages that will make your projects more likely to be done on time, within budget, and with high quality. The advantages of using these picture tools are that you and your team will be able to:

1. **Make sure the plan is realistic and agreed upon by the team** by viewing the plan from a unique perspective.

2. **Prepare for upcoming activities** so team members can keep the project moving ahead as planned.

3. **Concentrate attention** on the plan, so the project stays on schedule and within the budget.

4. **Anticipate bottlenecks before they occur**, so corrective action can minimize delays.

5. **Enhance coordination and communication** among the project team members.

6. **Build commitment** by publicly identifying responsibilities and deadlines and by creating awareness of interdependencies.

7. **Significantly increase the probability that projects are completed on time**, within budget, and with high quality.

To make the most of your planning efforts to this point, you have to create a picture of your **GOCART**. Supercharge the plan by capturing all of the information generated in the planning process in an easy-to-understand and easy-to-use picture. Use Gantt charts and PERT charts, along with some very powerful software programs to make your task easier (we do not focus on particular programs but encourage you to seek out ones available within your company).

As we show, creating these pictures can effectively galvanize and direct the energy of all team members. It is truly amazing how these charts generate a sense of responsibility among team members and unleash the energy and creativity to get the project done with outstanding success. Let's explore two types of charts you can use.

Understanding Gantt Charts

Gantt charts (named after Henry Gantt) have proved their usefulness again and again. They are simple to create, yet they capture a great deal of information about the project plan. They provide a useful overview of the project and constitute a quick management tool for monitoring project progress.

A Gantt chart has three basic parts: (1) a time line, (2) a list of activities, and (3) a bar for each activity (the length of which represents the time estimated for the activity and takes into account its relationship with other activities). Note that the list of activities, the relationships among activities, and the length of the bar (the time estimate) have already been established during the **GOCART** process. Now you are drawing a picture of these elements. At the top of the chart, you should include a statement of the goal (or objective, as appropriate), and you can also make note on the chart of important checkpoints (milestones) from your **GOCART** process. Figure 4.1 shows a partial Gantt chart for Noah's ark.

As you can see, Gantt charts provide an easy-to-read visual picture of all the elements of your project **GOCART**—checkpoints, activities, relationships, and time estimates. The end points of the bars mark checkpoints of progress. The length of the bars for each activity is proportional in length to the amount of time estimated for the activity. For example, "build vertical supports" is estimated to take 14 days and the bar is twice as long as that for "paint on leak filler," estimated to take 7 days. Gantt charts also show the sequencing of activities—those that must be completed before others and those that can or must be done at the same time. In the Gantt chart for Noah's ark, "nail on side slats" must be done before "paint on leak filler," but "build vertical supports" and "build horizontal supports" can be done at the same time (if there are sufficient resources to do so).

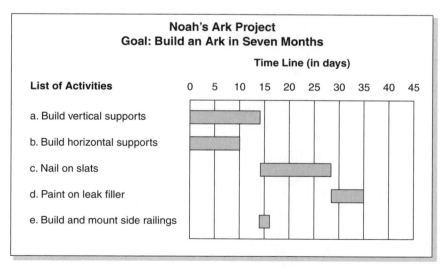

Figure 4.1 Part of a Gantt Chart for Noah's Ark

The familiar saying, "A picture is worth a thousand words" is certainly true in the case of a Gantt chart. These charts very quickly and effectively convey considerable information about a project. To ensure this easy-to-see application, you should confine a Gantt chart to one page so that you can visually take in an entire project (or section of the project for complex projects with vast numbers of activities).

In fact, a Gantt chart for a complex project typically collapses many activities together and shows only major events and milestones. The greater detail that has been created with the **GOCART** and that is needed to manage the project is conveyed in Gantt charts for each objective. These charts are then used by those responsible for this piece of the action plan. For example, on the ark project, Shem builds the vertical supports and the side railing and cuts the opening for the ramp. A Gantt chart of those activities helps him know what to do and when to do it. These additional Gantt charts help you coordinate the efforts of various people or groups working on different objectives. In this way you can begin to see the important interface points.

Gantt charts give everyone a quick and easy-to-understand
overview of the project.

You can also use the Gantt chart to analyze "What if?" situations and determine the best plan for a project. It is easy (especially with a computer program) to move the bars around on the chart to play with different options or to make contingency plans for "What could go wrong?" situations.

Furthermore, you can use the Gantt chart to track and monitor progress and to provide important feedback to team members. A common way of doing this is to shade in the bars to reflect the percentage of completion for an activity. Computer software programs make these updates relatively easy.

Take a look at the updated Gantt chart for the Ark Project (Figure 4.2). Point A on the time line reflects the current point in time. Combined with the shaded portion of the "build vertical supports" activity, it tells you that the project is right on schedule. If the shaded portion extends to the right beyond point A, as it does for "build horizontal supports," it means you are ahead of schedule. If the shaded portion does not extend to point A, it means you are behind schedule. At a glance, you can tell where you are in relation to the schedule. If you are on or ahead of sched-

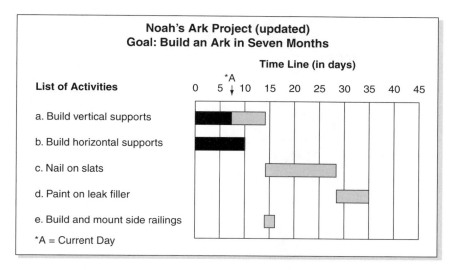

Figure 4.2 Partially Finished Project Shown on a Gantt Chart

ule, praise is called for; if you are behind, problem solving becomes a top priority. And since a Gantt chart allows you to spot problems early, it makes them easier to resolve.

Understanding PERT Charts

PERT (Program Evaluation and Review Technique) charts (also called CPM charts, for Critical Path Method) are another method for drawing a picture of a project schedule. They use the same information as the Gantt chart. Indeed, software packages provide both charts as outputs from one data input exercise. Of course, you may be wondering why you need two pictures of the same project plan. And the answer is that you do not, but PERT charts and Gantt charts display the information differently, and each has its advantages and disadvantages. PERT charts are not as easy to use as Gantt charts to show your progress to date on the project. But PERT charts are extremely useful in identifying and managing the sequential flow of critical activities in a project. On complex projects, it can be useful to use both types of charts.

Like the Gantt chart, a PERT chart has three basic components to depict elements from your **GOCART**: (1) lines to represent activities,

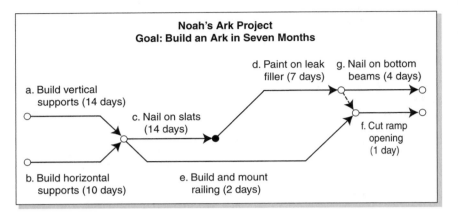

Figure 4.3 Part of a PERT Chart for Noah's Ark

(2) small circles or boxes to represent checkpoints, and (3) written-in time estimates. Figure 4.3 illustrates a partial PERT chart for Noah's ark (events are the hollow circles, milestones the shaded ones).

The "flow" of activities is readily apparent on a PERT chart (even more so than on a Gantt chart). It is clear, for example, that the vertical and horizontal supports must be completed on the ark before the side slats can be nailed on, whereas vertical and horizontal supports can be built at the same time. Also, all activities, events, milestones, and time estimates are easily accessible on the PERT chart. Use PERT charts to show the sequencing of activities for projects involving literally hundreds of activities.

This clear display of all project activities is one of the major advantage of a PERT chart over a Gantt chart. Another advantage of a PERT chart is its clear delination of the relationships and interfaces among activities. This feature is extremely valuable when two interfacing activities are done by two different people or teams. Coordination can be greatly enhanced through the PERT chart picture of the project plan.

> *PERT charts clearly show the sequencing of project*
> *activities, so the project team is less likely to waste*
> *time doing things out of order.*

Yet another advantage of a PERT chart is that you can easily determine the longest sequence of activities in the project by adding up the time estimates along each path through the project. The longest path is called the "critical path" because any delays on this path will delay the entire project. The length of the critical path determines the minimum amount of time for completing the project, since all paths must be completed before the project goal is achieved. The advantage of a PERT chart is that with software support, a project with hundreds of activities can be coordinated. However, a PERT chart with hundreds of activities can become confusing, so PERT charts are usually drawn in sections and separated into time blocks.

Working with Gantt and PERT Charts

Once PERT charts are created for a project, they greatly aid in daily planning and execution of work on the project. The Gantt chart provides the overview that is used for coordinating and integrating individual objectives into the overall project goals and for monitoring budget and resource allocations. In building the ark, for example, Noah might have used a PERT chart of the entire project and given pieces of it as Gantt charts to the carpenters, animal finders, food suppliers, and others. He might also have found a Gantt chart useful when apprising God of the ark's progress. It is not at all uncommon to see project managers using both types of charts to maximize the strengths of both.

Like a Gantt chart, a PERT chart can also be used to perform "What if?" analyses to determine the best plan for a project. Different charts can be drawn to represent alternative ways to complete the project. For each alternative chart, the times along the paths can be added to determine the critical path. "What if?" analysis may enable you to figure out a way to get the project done more quickly than was originally thought possible. One national restaurant chain used these techniques to significantly reduce the project completion time on store conversion. The typical conversion cycle had been six months. But after purchasing 150 stores from other restaurant chains, senior management knew they could not take that long for each conversion. By drawing pictures (Gantt and PERT charts) of the conversion and then moving boxes and arrows around, they could perform "What if?" analyses and were able to reduce the conversion cycle by over 50 percent.

Using a PERT chart for "What could go wrong?" analyses can help you determine the impact on the project of a delay in any activity. You simply push the delay through the project to determine its impact. Often, delays will have minimal impact on overall project completion, because only delays on the longest path cause delays in project completion. Other paths have slack, since their total time estimates are less than that for the longest path. It is true, however, that enough delays on a noncritical path can convert it into a critical path.

You can see how a PERT chart can help in managing a project by examining the partial PERT chart for Noah's ark in Figure 4.4. Of the seven possible paths on the PERT chart, the one in bold arrows is the longest (49 days). This part of the project cannot be completed in less than 49 days. The other paths are shorter and hence have slack (extra time). For example, the path from "build horizontal supports" through "build and mount side railings" through "cut opening for ramp" is 22 days long. This means that delays of up to 27 days (49–22) can be tolerated on this path before the project completion date will be delayed.

Note also the dashed-line activity connecting "paint on leak filler" and "cut ramp opening." It has no name and no time attached. It is called a "dummy activity," and it is needed to show relationships in special cases. Here, for example, "Cut ramp opening" depends on both "build and mount side railings" and "paint on leak filler," but "nail on bottom support beams" depends only on "paint on leak filler." The dummy activity allows this set of relationships to be made clear.

With the PERT chart in Figure 4.4 you can calculate the earliest time you expect to be ready to begin each activity, as well as the latest time you can begin each activity and still complete the project on schedule. If you add times for activities along a path moving left to right, you get the earliest start times. For example, adding the 14 days for "activity a," the 14 days for "activity c," and the 7 days for "activity d," you learn that the earliest start date for "activity f" is 35 days. Fortunately, such calculations can be handled quite easily by computer programs.

To calculate the latest possible start time for each activity (which still keeps the project on schedule) the software works backward (right to left) in the chart, subtracting activity times from the overall project time. For example, we said this project's critical path is 49 days long. By subtracting the 2 days for "activity k," then the 7 days for "activity h," and the 1 day for "activity f," we learn that the latest start date for "activity f" is 39 days. Given the 35 days earliest start date for "activity f," we find that there are 4 days of slack for this activity. For activities on the critical path these calculations will reveal zero days of slack for the Ark Project.

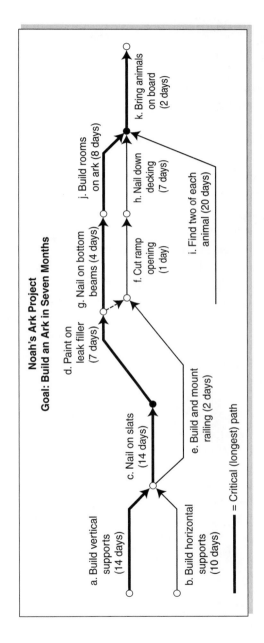

Figure 4.4 A PERT Chart Example

As with the Gantt chart, you can update a PERT chart regularly to reflect actual progress on the project. This is especially useful when determining how changes will affect the overall project completion time and also for managing interfaces between various people and departments. Such updates are essential for maintaining the power of your project supercharger tools, and updates do require some discipline on your part. Is it worth the time? Definitely—if you want to be a winning project leader!

Getting Projects Back on Track

Perhaps one of the most useful aspects of PERT charts and Gantt charts is in steering projects back on schedule when they fall behind. For example, slack on a particular path may indicate underutilized resources. Sometimes these resources can be shifted to the longest path to speed things along. However, be careful not to shift so many resources that a noncritical path falls behind schedule and becomes a critical path. In the Noah's ark project, it is clear that there is slack on the "nail down decking" path (see Figure 4.4). Perhaps these people could help build rooms on the ark if problems are encountered.

A related way to steer projects back on track is to shift slack time. Consider using the slack at the beginning, in the middle, or at the end of an activity. Noah, for example, could find the animals early in the project and hold them in a pen. Meanwhile, some of the animal finders could help on other paths of the project.

Of course, you can allocate overtime, add shifts, or bring in subcontractors to help bring projects back on schedule, but you must monitor costs to keep them under control. The key here is to use your PERT charts and Gantt charts to help you consider alternatives. By being creative and conducting "What if we did it this way?" discussions, you can use the Gantt charts and PERT charts to analyze these alternatives and bring the project in on time, within budget, and with high quality.

A Note on Computer Software

As we have noted, drawing and using project pictures for planning, modifying, contingency planning, and updating is made far easier by the many easy-to-use software packages available today. But do not make the mistake of thinking the software can create your **GOCART** for you. It cannot set goals or objectives, nor can it define checkpoints, activities, relationships, and time estimates. The project team must do these things before the computer can Supercharge the **GOCART** by drawing a useful picture of the schedule. And for simple projects, resorting to the computer software is probably not even worth the trouble.

> *Computer software for projects is only a tool*
> *to assist you—it cannot think for you.*

Developing a **GOCART** is the responsibility for you and the team. Once you have a **GOCART**, computer software and its picture creation capability can Supercharge that plan for action. And this supercharger will be of real value in creating passion and responsibility for every team member. The result: you and your project team will win the race and take home the coveted checkered flag!

Summary

Rule Four:
Supercharge the Plan with a Picture

1. Gantt charts and PERT charts are two common and useful methods you can use to draw a picture of your project **GOCART** and to aid in staying on schedule.

2. Gantt charts are visually compelling and provide a quick overview of a project, thus enabling team members to easily monitor progress.

3. PERT charts are more complex than Gantt charts, but they help you to clarify and manage the sequential flow of critical activities on a project.

4. By working with Gantt and PERT charts, you can develop a highly effective project plan. Continuing to use these charts during the project facilitates on-time, on-budget, and high-quality completion of the project goal.

5. Numerous software packages are available to aid you in depicting your plan and managing its progress.

6. Your **GOCART** can now be **S**upercharged to help you win the race.

> **G**oal clarified
>   **O**bjectives and responsibilities defined
>   **C**heckpoints established
>   **A**ctivities established
>   **R**elationships established
>   **T**ime (cost) estimates set
>   **S**upercharged with a picture

Congratulations! You now have the tools to build a Supercharged **GOCART** for your projects. And you are ready to develop the **DRIVER** skills that will take your **GOCART** to the checkered flag.

Rule Five: Develop an Empowered Project Team

There is a limit to what I can do by myself, but unlimited potential for us as an empowered team!

Thus far we have focused on the importance of developing a great plan for a winning project. By following the steps in the **GOCART-S** process, you can develop a vehicle for project success, but a well-designed plan will not get the job done unless you also have the skills for managing the plan. Your **GOCART** needs a **DRIVER** (our acronym for the skills of a winning project leader). Beginning in this chapter, we focus attention on six skills for effective management of a project plan. We start with the "D" in **DRIVER**—**D**evelop an Empowered Project Team.

The most basic, fundamental, and often overlooked rule about successful project management is: "You can't do it alone!" Alone, you may enjoy a single lap in the lead, but not likely a victory at the end of the race. Individuals may win awards, but it is teams that win championships. Time and again studies reveal that projects fail because the project leader has not built a strong team. This generally happens because the project leader is unable to tap into the talents and energy of all members of the project team. This inability (and often unwillingness) to draw out the potential contributions of others in a collective fashion is one of the primary reason projects fail. As Ken Blanchard and his colleagues say in *The One Minute Manager Builds High Performing Teams,* "None of us is as smart as all of us."

To be a winner as a project leader, you have to build an *empowered project team*—a team that:

1. Asks for, uses, and shares information

2. Functions autonomously within boundaries

3. Creates a synergy of effort, talent, and skill

4. Seeks out responsibility

5. Makes and implements decisions

6. Shares risks and rewards with project leaders

7. Takes great pride in what they accomplish

In working to develop an empowered project team, you need to know about the predictable issues that will arise as teams travel through the various stages of development. In addition, you need to know how to address these issues to keep the team moving forward. What makes it difficult to develop an empowered team is that people are very complex, and putting them together in an interdependent team significantly adds to that complexity. Let us provide some building blocks for developing an empowered team.

We start by using the basics of human behavior to look first at yourself as the project leader. Next we learn how to gain an understanding of other people and their unique and diverse aspects. Finally, we put it all together by exploring the issues and stages of team development.

Know Yourself

To understand how to best work with others to create an empowered project team, you need to understand your own competencies and motivational forces. Reflect upon your experiences to date, and try to be realistic about what you can and cannot do well. Also, think about what aspects of project management excite and motivate you and which ones you hate to do. There are numerous questions to ponder:

- Where have you been victorious?
- What contributed to your success?
- How did you feel in these successful situations?
- When have you been disappointed?
- What would you do differently now?
- Can you articulate the lessons you have learned from your life, from the peaks as well as the valleys?

> *To understand what makes other people tick, first understand yourself. What makes you hum with energy? What are you really good at doing?*

For example, when you complete each project, take time to ask for feedback from the team. Ask questions like: "What did we learn?" "How could we have accomplished this better?" and "What should I do similarly or differently next time?" Asking such questions leads to an accumulation of experiential learning, rather than ten years of experience being the result of one year's experience repeated ten times. Sports teams, for example, review their performance after each game—not just at the end of the season.

Through post-project reviews you can learn what you as project leader did well so that you can incorporate these methods into future projects. You can also make note of things that did not work out well, so that you can avoid these mistakes in the future. Otherwise, "project amnesia" will likely doom you to repeating the same mistakes over and over. Learning does take time and effort, but if learning occurs, things will be better next time.

Another benefit from enhanced self-awareness is that you begin to understand and appreciate the vast array of reasons why other people do what they do. People who are clueless about the reasons for their own behavior have little basis upon which to frame ideas about what makes others behave as they do. But you must be very careful not to let your experiences create blinders that limit your appreciation of your team members. Often we see what we expect to see rather than what is actually occurring. Expectations are powerful because they form frames into which we fit others' behavior. If we believe that some people on the project are lazy, we will interpret their behaviors as lazy. Only behavior that is clearly contrary to our expectations will cause us to change the way we see things. And even then we are likely to be unhappy about changing, because it means we have to admit (even if only to ourselves) that we made a mistake!

Further, when we behave toward others according to the way we expect them to respond (for example, closely supervising those we predict will be lazy), they often will act as we expect—because *our* behavior shapes a self-fulfilling prophecy. In effect, our actions create the situation we expect, thus reinforcing our initial perception and limiting what the other person can contribute. It is critical to take the time to appreciate how others act to satisfy their own needs.

Know Others: All Behavior Makes Sense

To understand the behavior of your team members, let us begin by considering their capabilities. Have you ever done anything in your life that was stupid? Most of us would have to say yes (at least once). But when we reflect on that foolish behavior, did we act that way because we intended to be stupid or foolish? Certainly not. To understand another person's potentially stupid behavior, we need to examine it from that person's point of view. We need to ask the question "How does this behavior make sense to that person?" By using this perspective, we can be analytical and descriptive about what people are doing rather than evaluative and general.

Remember that your perception of reality is not always the same as someone else's. For example, it may seem stupid to you that engineering has not released the design plans, even though they are completed and already two months past due. But it makes sense to the engineers because they believe that their appeal for additional staff will be stronger if it appears that they need more personnel (that is, it takes so long to complete design plans). Or consider how it makes perfect sense and seems only fair to you when you leave the office a few hours early on Friday. After all, you'll be back in again on Saturday, and the company "owes" you some time off with your family. But to other project team members, this behavior appears wrong because your departure suggests a lack of real commitment to the project.

Just imagine God saying to Noah, "Noah, what are you doing getting the animals together before the ark is completed? Are you crazy?" And Noah saying, "Wait a minute, what I'm trying to do is . . . ." Each person needs to understand the perspectives of other team members if the team is to work together effectively.

Know Others: All People Are Motivated

Team members operate off more than capabilities. Work output depends also on people's motivation. Have you ever met an unmotivated person? Most of us agree that we have. But, this is a trick question. If unmotivated people exist, then individual behavior would have to be random and capricious—and behavior is neither. As we discussed, all actions make sense to the person doing the acting. When you respond affirmatively to this question, what you are thinking about is a person who is motivated to do something other than what you want that person to do. All people are motivated. The question is: "Motivated to do what?" Consequently, it is only from our perspective, and not theirs, that they are not motivated. You should think about motivation as the area of overlap between project goals and individual goals.

All people are motivated. The question is: "Motivated to do what?"

All behavior is directed toward the satisfaction of individual needs. If you find out more about the needs, desires, wants, and goals of the members of your project team, you will have some chance of motivating their behavior—assuming that you can help them satisfy their needs.

Knowing a team member's needs is crucial because needs that are already satisfied do not motivate or influence people's behavior. It is difficult, for example, to motivate state-of-the-art engineers by threatening to fire them when they can easily go out and find another job. Furthermore, people do not focus on higher-level needs when their lower-level needs are not being met. For instance, it would be hard to encourage more innovation from a marketing group whose members are worried about losing their jobs, being relocated, or being phased out.

Know Others: People Are Unique

Creating an effective project team means coalescing a mixture of talents and motivations. The dilemma you face is in this paradox: People share commonalities, but people are unique in the talents and motivations they bring to the team. Although this proposition is obviously true, the way it translates into behavior is often very subtle. Maintaining a balance between treating everyone on the team the same (or managing everyone consistently) and being sensitive to individual differences is not easy. We see this effectively implemented when project leaders treat individuals with respect and dignity while coordinating their activities with consistency and continuity.

Everyone has interests, goals, and a personality, but each person's interests, goals, and personality are unique. You face the challenge of balancing consistency and equity in relating to people. Dealing with the different personalities on a project team or task force requires considerable skill and often much ingenuity. In addition, the challenge of motivating the efforts of the people on your project team is complicated because people do not behave consistently over time, probably because no two situations are ever exactly alike. An understanding of the perceptual process helps to explain this. Simply put, we behave in terms of our perception of reality, and that perception is determined partly by what's outside us and partly by what's inside us.

Perceptual differences can readily influence the ways in which project team members respond to organizational and managerial practices. Different individuals, for example, vary in terms of the importance they attach to job-related rewards, the style of leadership they prefer, their need for interpersonal contact and interaction, and their tolerance and acceptance of job responsibility.

For example, could Noah treat everyone working on the ark the same way? If he told his associates that they were doing a good job, one might be flattered, while another might wonder about what was wrong with the way he had been working. Still another might be suspicious of Noah's motives ("Does he mean it or is he just trying to flatter me before asking me to work overtime?").

Neither Noah nor you can treat everyone identically, even if you want to. Some people may have a greater need to know that their work is being appreciated than others do. Some will want less variety in their routines, while others will seek out new challenges. Different people must be treated differently.

> *There is nothing so unequal as the equal treatment of unequals.*

The implications for you as a project leader are clear. Don't expect other people to see things exactly as you would view them, no matter how clear things seem to you and how certain you are about the accuracy of your point of view. Expect differences among team members as well, since each person filters the same information through a different screen. Be prepared to spend time talking with project team members. Ask what energizes them, ask what makes their tasks meaningful, find out what they want from this project, and watch for the things that excite them. Use this knowledge to make sense of why they behave as they do. Expect to take time and effort to mold a team from the diverse set of individual team members, especially if you want an empowered project team.

Know How to Create an Empowered Project Team

Understanding yourself and the other people on the project team is essential for molding an empowered team. However, the group of people who work together on a project do not automatically become a team the day the project begins. It takes time and energy to convert a group of people into an empowered team that can synergistically apply their talents, differences, and energy in a way that achieves astonishing results on the project. A group of individuals must pass together through several stages of evolution as they address the issues in becoming a team. Appreciating these stages and learning how to address the issues raised in the stages will definitely increase your chances of being a winning project leader.

Stage One—Orientation. When a project team is first selected and brought together during the early stage of the project cycle (where the goal and objectives are being set), they are a set of individuals, each with their own perspectives, motivations, and talents. All the potential may be there for these people to become a very effective team, but they are not yet a "team." During this *orientation* stage of team development, the team members wonder what the project is really about and what their roles will be. They have some anxiety about how this team will work, as compared to others they have worked with before. In short, there is a certain level of confusion that you must reduce if the team is to pass through this developmental stage. For example, Noah had to clarify for the group why the ark was to be built, as well as to overcome their skepticism about Noah really talking to God. By doing so, he was able to move the group beyond orientation.

> *A group of people just working together doesn't constitute an empowered project team.*

Stage Two—Dissatisfaction. Interestingly enough, the second stage of team development is perhaps the most difficult and develops naturally as an outgrowth of Stage One. By clarifying the goal and objectives as well as the team member roles, the project leader creates a gap between reality and the initial expectations of the team members. Not everything is as the team members naïvely thought it would be when they joined the project, and this leads the group into the *dissatisfaction* stage of team development. Team members may be heard to say, "This is not what I thought it would be like." Or "What have we gotten ourselves into now?" Sounds bad, right? Maybe you can think of times you have experienced these issues on project teams before; indeed, some teams never recover from this stage of development.

Unfortunately, this stage of dissatisfaction often occurs just as the team needs to kick the project into high gear and move forward with implementation. Figure 5.1 shows the relationship between stages of team development and stages of the project life. Just when the resource utilization is starting to move up, the team hits a drop in team energy and team competence is still relatively low. As project leader, you must expect and embrace this stage of team development. Hard work is required to guide the team through this stage, as they develop and refine both their team competence and team energy. This stage of dissatisfaction is necessary in order to bring about a sense of empowerment in a project team, but it is clearly an uncomfortable stage. What team members need is someone to blame (for example, the project leader!), but what they also need is someone to provide continued direction and encouragement. Listen to their concerns, respond appropriately, and keep providing clari-

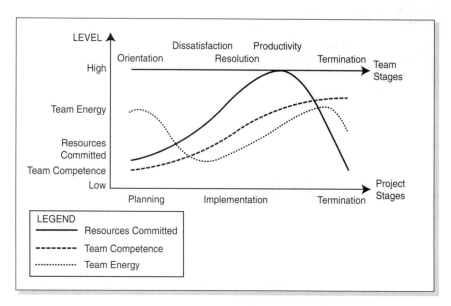

Figure 5.1 Project Stages versus Team Development Stages

ty about what is required to get the job done. There is life after this stage if you can lead the team through it.

Stage Three—Resolution. From the pits of dissatisfaction a properly managed group will begin to grow into a team, but a team that still has a way to go to become an empowered team. As the team members develop the ability and energy to work together, they are entering the *resolution* stage of development. You can even feel it as the team begins to develop a sense of cohesion. As Figure 5.1 shows, team competence and team energy are rising, as the need for project resources nears its peak, so it is critical to keep the team moving toward empowerment. This third stage is a delicate time, though, and teams often shy away from necessary conflict during the resolution stage. They do not want to go back into the uncomfortable dissatisfaction stage again. So you need to continue to provide encouragement, but the encouragement needs to push the group to take risks and to work through, rather than avoid, disagreements. Noah might say to his team, "Do we really want to put the lions with the sheep?" thus helping the team deal with a potential problem. The team, without this helpful nudge, might not address this problem, only to have it erupt once the ark is loaded with animals.

Stage Four—Productivity. Eventually and long before the project ends, a well-managed group of people can become an empowered project team as they move into the stage of *productivity*. In this stage, the team provides its own direction and encouragement, deals constructively with conflicts, and acts responsibly to complete its assignments. In fact, in this stage your focus is on getting the team the resources and recognition that it needs. The project can proceed toward the goal on time, within budget, and with quality, because team members can work together to get it done on their own. But remember that getting to this stage of productivity takes time, proper management of the issues of each previous stage of development, and an understanding of the overall process of team development. At this stage of development, Noah would likely be focusing his energy of dealing with God (". . . and just when will the rains begin, and how quickly, and . . . ."). Without distractions, the team members can get their job done more efficiently.

Stage Five—Termination. One final caveat: as the project team nears the completion of the project, you must consider the *termination* stage. When the project end comes into sight, some team members may slack off in their efforts because they feel the project is almost over. Often, they will need a nudging (gentle) along with a reminder about the importance of meeting the schedule with a completed project. Some team members may even experience sadness and a sense of loss about the team's impending demise. These folks require encouragement and emotional understanding.

Stage Postview. In each of these five stages, the key question to keep asking is: "What does the team need now to deal with current issues and keep moving through the stages of development?" How much direction and guidance do they need? How much support and encouragement do they need? Do they need both direction and support, or do they need high on one and low on the other, or perhaps low on both direction and support? Proper analysis and follow-through can transform a group of people into a high-performing, empowered team that can help the project win.

Summary

Rule Five:
Develop an Empowered Project Team

1. To manage teams successfully, you must understand the elements of human behavior: first your own, then the behavior of members of your team.

2. Miscommunication often results from a clash of perspectives. Learn how other people perceive their goals. Remember, all behavior makes sense to the behaving person.

3. Every team member is likely to be motivated by something different. A critical task of the team leader is to recognize and reward the correct motivators for each team member.

4. As a team leader, appreciate and promote the differences of team members and how they contribute uniquely to project goal achievement.

5. Teams are not made in an instant. To reach the desired stage of high productivity and empowerment, teams must first go through the stages of orientation, dissatisfaction, and resolution, even as they simultaneously move through the stages of the project life. As the project nears completion, the stage of termination must also be managed.

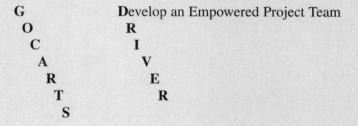

Rule Six: Reinforce People's Motivation and Energy

People don't wash rental cars!

An essential element in managing a winning project is reflected in the "**R**" in **DRIVER**—**R**einforce the internal motivation and energy of people about the project. As we discussed in Rule Five, everyone is motivated; the question is, motivated to do what. If you can tap into people's internal motivation and energy and then direct it toward the project goal, you have a powerful force working for your project. People on the project team will not simply "do their job"; they will embrace the project with a passion that yields astonishing results. You don't just have their eyes, ears, and hands; you also have their hearts and minds. Think about the difference between working with people who are in their jobs "for something to do" versus those who are in their jobs "to do something."

Several years ago a special project group in one of our clients was assigned the task of designing a new computer. The project manager used special rituals to get people excited and committed to the project. For example, every member of the project team passed through an initiation rite called "signing up." In joining the project team, a person agreed to do

67

whatever was necessary to make the project succeed. This could mean forsaking family, friends, hobbies, and all vestiges of a nonwork life until the project was completed.

The reasons behind this ritual were simple. People who make this kind of commitment to a project no longer need to be coerced to work on it. They have volunteered. Indeed, the best predictor of project success is often whether the project participants have volunteered for the project. Your challenge as a project leader is to create the ambiance of volunteers even when people have been assigned to the project.

If the people on your task force or project were
volunteers, would you treat them differently?

The project leader with our client went to great lengths to get an unusually high degree of commitment to the computer design project; you will not always need this kind of commitment to a job. You will, however, need to make sure that your project team is behind the project, working in the same direction to achieve the project's goals, rather than in front of the project, acting as roadblocks to progress. To accomplish this, you need to do more than lay out the project goals and objectives and issue instructions about what to do. You need to make team members feel that they are participating in an exciting venture, guided by a shared vision of how their efforts will bring success. Some of your efforts and the process associated with building your project **GOCART** will have set in motion these dynamics. Now is the time to keep the energy flowing in the right direction—toward project completion on time, within budget, and with high quality.

Imagine the initial project meetings between Noah and his team. Noah says, "OK, who wants to help build the ark?" Pause. "Well, what do you mean by an ark?" asks one person. Another says, "Noah, why do you think an ark is needed? Who told you it's going to rain?" "What do you want us to do?" says a third person.

Drawing upon people's internal motivation requires that you make certain everyone understands what the project is all about and how they can contribute to its accomplishment; think back to the process of setting a project goal and related objectives and the idea of creating a passion for the project. To successfully reach the finish line of the project as a winner, you must continually reinforce this passion by tapping into the internal motivation and related energy within people. Let's look at these two key elements.

Drawing upon Internal Motivation

Researchers have demonstrated the ways that companies and managers build strong organizational cultures that can help maintain high levels of commitment and internal work motivation for a project. Basic to this process is being clear about key corporate values, building consensus around them, and making certain that people feel responsible for the project's success.

Excellent companies and high-performing teams develop and are guided by clearly articulated values about how they intend to run their businesses, programs, or projects. This clarity creates a shared belief among people that focusing and adhering to these values will bring them success. Research has shown that commitment, loyalty, and pride, as well as organizational productivity, are directly related to the clarity, consensus, and intensity of organizational values and standards. Correspondence between personal and organizational values significantly affects levels of individual motivation, willingness to work hard, concern for clients and customers, and levels of job satisfaction and effectiveness.

Making full use of the intelligence of project members is essential to the success of any project team or self-directed work team. Achieving high quality depends on a recognition that employees at all levels have good ideas about how to improve productivity and that managers can benefit by using these ideas. People who work on effective projects feel empowered to own problems and to fix them in the best way they can. Do people on your project teams own problems and fix them, drawing on their skills, experience, and internal motivation? If not, why not?

More and more companies today are turning to self-managed work teams. These teams are not subject to many of the traditional managerial controls. Indeed, the teams act as managers themselves. The teams are given considerable autonomy to make their own decisions, as if they are a small business themselves rather than submerged in a larger company. The teams are given fairly broad goals but freedom to use their ideas and motivation to determine how to achieve them. They tap the intelligence and abilities of team members to tackle numerous projects that greatly enhance their productive capabilities. The results have often been dramatic, with productivity increases of 30 to 40 percent and more.

So here's the point. Create a sense of empowerment and ownership, and you will see people owning and fixing problems. When you rent a car, do you get it washed? No! And the reason is that the car is not yours, you are not the owner. Taking care of the car is clearly the job of the rental company. Project teams achieve the best results when members feel ownership, when they are empowered to contribute their own ideas to the project and to share responsibility for making important decisions. These conditions give project team members the opportunity to experience their work as meaningful. Surveys show that this is a critical motivator for professionals today.

Internal motivation is tapped when people feel
a sense of ownership and empowerment.

Building and Maintaining Energy

To drive your projects past the waving checkered flag, you must provide opportunities to "encourage the heart" of the members of your project team. Don't make the mistake of assuming that only money excites individuals. Although increases in salary or bonuses are certainly appreciated, effort based on financial reward is often short-lived. You can't buy people's energy. Successful project leaders can be distinguished from less effective leaders by their greater use of creative (and nonfinancial) incentives. Verbal recognition of performance in front of one's peers and visible awards, such as certificates, plaques, and other tangible gifts, are powerful ways to get people's attention.

For example, one senior bank officer placed a large bell in the middle of the office. Every time someone made a loan, he or she got to ring it. At a national retail company, top executives send out note cards that have "I heard something good about you" printed at the top. They send them not just to other officers but also to clerks, buyers, trainees, and other line employees. "Sticker redemption parties" are held at a large manufacturing company. Employees receive stickers for "extra effort" and these stickers can be redeemed at month's end for food and beverages at the party.

Such actions may appear silly and unnecessary, but they provide a healthy opportunity for people to recognize and share their success with others—and they are fun. More important though, such celebrations encourage shared visions of both what needs to be done and why it is important. They also reinforce more strongly than financial rewards that challenging goals can be realized through individual and collective efforts. In effect, you get both the benefit of individual energy and collective team energy, as we discussed in Rule Five. You need to constantly look for ways to spread the psychological benefits of making people feel like winners. Winners contribute in important ways to the success of their projects, and most people on the project team can be winners, given the chance. And guess what? If your team members are winners, your project will pick up the checkered flag, and you will be a winning project leader.

Tapping People's Motivation and Energy

There are many ways to tap into the internal motivation and energy of the people on your project team. Here are five of the most successful:

1. Create challenging possibilities.

2. Inspire a shared vision.

3. Increase visibility.

4. Empower people.

5. Spread the "praises" around.

1. **Create challenging possibilities** by giving people the big picture and by promoting the meaningfulness of their efforts. As we discussed in Rule One, make sure everyone on the project knows and stays focused on the overall project goal. "We're trying to build an ark that will save us from the flood. Don't lose sight of how each board you nail on will help keep the ark afloat." Your people need to know at the outset not only what they are trying to accomplish but for whom and why. To do otherwise is to foster the alienation and apathy of "it's just another job!"

   The project leaders at one of our clients go to considerable effort to give every team member an understanding of the company's business and five-year plan. They want people to see the big picture to which their efforts will contribute. Studies show that when people understand why they are being asked to do something they are more likely to cooperate. Have you noticed the signs appearing at many zoos, replacing the traditional signs around the animal cage that used to read "Please stand three feet from the cage" with ones marked "Animals spit"? Notice any changes in where people stand relative to the cages? Letting people see the big picture boosts motivation and energy.

2. **Inspire a shared vision** of the project's purpose and goal. Your job is to create a vision of what's possible and then to show others how their own aspirations can be aligned with those of the project. When the project goal is a shared vision among the project team members, they are more likely to be committed, loyal, productive, willing to put in the necessary time, and much less hassled and tense. Also, they are more willing to use their motivation, energy, and intelligence for the common good. Evidence of this dedication is the T-shirt worn by members of one product development group: "Working 90 hours a week and loving it."

   Noah's own faith in God's prophecy helped to convince others to build the ark. You cannot overemphasize the project's goal and its importance. Frequent conversations about the project (e.g., status updates) are essential. Keeping people posted helps to sustain their focus. Listening and dealing with their concerns while keeping everyone focused on the shared vision emphatically reinforces the "we're in this together" level of commitment. As many effective project leaders have noted, "There is no I in the word TEAM!" Joint effort is essential for project success.

3. **Increase visibility** of the project team's efforts. Part of the magic behind schedules (Gantt and PERT charts) is that they are public. They make visible the commitments of each member of the project. They make people accountable and provide ongoing feedback about results. They also provide information about critical interdependencies. Without this sense of interdependency, the people on your project team may not be motivated to cooperate with one another or feel a shared sense of responsibility and fate.

   For example, visibility contributes to the psychological glue that holds most religious groups together. Members regularly demonstrate publicly their beliefs together with their peers. You need to "get religion" for your team by making project team members' efforts visible to one another. Some companies use an "info center" to supply everyone with the detailed information given only to top managers at many companies. Everybody knows what everyone else is doing and is supposed to be doing. Hence everyone can act responsibly; everyone can cooperate more effectively. And everyone can help hold one another accountable for results that benefit the overall project goal.

4. **Empower people** to be effective by using their intelligence and natural drive. Empowering others means giving them the information, resources, and authority necessary to make things happen. Give your project team the chance to perform. Give them the data, the goals, and the freedom to operate. Successful project leaders know that "giving away power" in this empowering fashion does not reduce their own power. On the contrary, as one hospital administrator exclaimed: "Since I've started being more empowering as a leader, I've never had so much power myself." This premise has been well tested. Effective project leaders find that empowering others—sharing information and responsibility—results in more committed and more engaged project team members. Work get done more easily because you are tapping people's internal motivation, knowledge, and experience.

> *Putting power and responsibility in the hands of your team members is like investing in a solid and growing company. It is guaranteed to pay big dividends.*

With these actions you also demonstrate your trust in other people's competence. You build their self-confidence and tap into their internal self-esteem, which is a most powerful performance motivator.

5. **Spread the "praises" around** to show appreciation and to show off people's accomplishments. Seldom do people complain that they are thanked too much by their managers. The checkpoints we discussed in Rule Three should mark times for celebration. People want to be effective, they want to be noticed, and they want to be appreciated. Successful project leaders understand that people want to be winners. People don't begin each day with a desire to lose. It is part of your job to show people that they can

win. A key characteristic of outstanding team leaders is the exuberance with which they celebrate accomplishments. Spreading the good word about the accomplishments of your team members will increase their visibility and enhance their own power and reputation. Some of the credit will inevitably find its way back to you. Your ability to evoke people's excitement and commitment will be noticed.

Reinforcing the internal motivation and energy of the project team means drawing from a deep reservoir within people. Motivation is tricky because you don't really motivate others. Rather, you invite and allow people's motivation to be directed toward project goals. The unfortunate truth is that the average project member uses only 30 percent or so of his or her potential. By following the ideas given here, you can begin to tap into the other 70 percent. The payoff will be amazing. People will work just as hard when you are not around as when you are there. Your project will get done on time, within budget, and with quality. Your **GOCART-S** will be the winner that brings home the checkered flag!

Summary

Rule Six:
Reinforce People's Motivation and Energy

1. Build both a sense of commitment to the goal and excitement about the project by encouraging team members to "own" the project.

2. Give people the big picture. Make sure that your project is not viewed as just "another job" but rather as a challenging possibility.

3. Align people's values and interests, both with one another and with the project goal. Be the spark that ignites the fire in others.

4. Share information and authority so that people believe you trust them to do the job. Responsibility without the necessary resources and authority has always been a recipe for disaster.

5. Enhance internal motivation and energy by making people's actions (and accomplishments) visible to others. Be a cheerleader because there is no such thing as a cheer-manager.

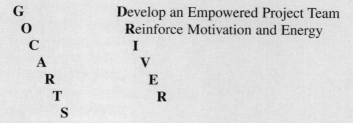

```
G                 Develop an Empowered Project Team
   O                 Reinforce Motivation and Energy
      C                 I
         A                 V
            R                 E
               T                 R
                  S
```

Rule Seven:
Inform
Everyone
Regularly

No good idea ever entered the head through an open mouth.

Keeping all project stakeholders and the people on your team **I**nformed is essential to the success of any project. The "**I**" in the **DRIVER** acronym reminds us of the crucial role information plays in getting the best performance out of your **GOCART-S** and the empowered team you have developed. Unfortunately, most of us do not communicate as effectively as we should. We do not regularly inform people on the project team, upper management, our colleagues, our end users, and even sometimes ourselves. Communication problems are experienced more often than anyone would like to admit. Have you ever experienced the kind of communication problem depicted in Figure 7.1, where everyone views the same issue from a different perspective? Many of us do all too often. But stop for a minute and think about why this happens.

As Marketing requested it

As Sales ordered it

As Engineering designed it

As Data Processing programmed it

As Services installed it

What the Customer ordered

Figure 7.1 Communication breakdowns make meaningful communications difficult. (From Sathre, Olson, and Whitney, *Let's Talk: An Introduction to Interpersonal Communications*, 2nd ed., © 1981. Reprinted/adapted by permission of Allyn & Bacon.)

Barriers to Effective Information Flow

In this era of amazing information technology, we would think that communications and information flows should also be amazing. Everyone has
Internet access, mobile phones, faxes, electronic organizers, portable
computers, and on and on. But are you communicating better today than
you did a few years ago, when you had fewer technological options?
Most people tell us "no." They spend lots of time checking e-mail, voicemail, mobile phones, their organizers, etc., but they do not really communicate any better. Why?

If you think about it, you can probably come up with quite a list of
reasons why communication problems exist. Most of these reasons fall
into one of two types of barriers: personal and organizational.

Personal barriers include such things as emotions, preoccupation,
hostility, past experiences, hidden agendas, inarticulateness, stereotyping,
physical environment (like machine noise and telephone interruptions),
daydreaming, defensiveness, and information overload.

For example, Noah's woodcutters might say, "Those carpenters
wouldn't know a good board if they saw one. They're all stupid" (stereotyping). Or the thunder is crackling as they try to finish the ark. Noah
says, "God, I can't hear you" (noise). Unfortunately, project team members often place greater emphasis on these personal barriers than they
should. How many times have you heard "We just have a personality conflict," as though there were no hope for solution short of banishing one or
both of the team members?

The fact is that organizational barriers are often much more important than personality differences in creating communication problems.
Many barriers originate from the very nature of a project team, which
typically involves people from different departments. Team members use
different languages, have different objectives, have had different types of
training, and yet must work together closely on a unique task to accomplish a common goal. Organizational barriers to communications also
include the following:

- Organizational structures that typically separate departments, both
  geographically and psychologically

- Information overload or, sometimes, information underload (too
  little information)

- Ambiguity leading to incomplete information or faulty transmission of information

- Time pressures

With projects, organizational barriers to communication are
often much more important than personal barriers.

For example, Noah's woodcutters cannot communicate with his animal handlers because of language differences. The trunks of animals are quite different from the trunks of trees, yet the word used to describe them (trunk) is the same. Kiln-dried wood, though of critical importance to woodcutters, may not mean anything to the animal handlers. And aren't the animal selectors the most important players on the team? If you have any doubts, just ask them.

This example illustrates how the nature of your job affects your communications and problem-solving approach. Generally, manufacturing and operations personnel have short time horizons because the outcome of their work (productivity) can be measured relatively quickly and definitively (e.g., units per hour). However, the time horizons for their counterparts in such areas as software engineering, new product development, and research are much longer. You would not measure the productivity of personnel in these functions by lines of code per hour, new products per week, or even patents per month. So, when your project team brings together people from design backgrounds and people from operations, the different team members will have vastly different senses of urgency and importance for many tasks on the project. And these differences can create real problems since people's tasks are interdependently connected.

You could probably add several more barriers to either list, but the real issue is what you can do to overcome the barriers to communication. In focusing on what to do to improve information sharing, it is helpful to go back to the basics of communication. In every situation, there is the sending of a message and the receiving of that message on the other end. If we use these basic aspects of communication, we can focus on two critical questions for improvement. First, what do you need to do to get your message across more effectively? Second, what do you need to do to be a better listener when you are on the receiving end?

Getting Your Message Across Effectively

As the sender of a message, cultivate the knack for getting the other person to listen to what you are saying. Four basic practices can help you improve communications and get your message across, regardless of what medium you are using to send the message:

1. Craft the message to appeal to others where they are (not where you wish they were).

2. Strive to help the receiver know why your message is important to him or her.

3. Keep others on the project team and stakeholders regularly informed.

4. Communicate assertively and with understanding.

1. **Craft the message to appeal to others where they are.** Make it your business to know and appreciate what is on other people's minds. What needs or problems are they thinking about? What words, phrases, examples, or analogies will make the most sense to them? What is the best medium to use from the perspective of the other people—do they like e-mail, voicemail, or face-to-face? Often, you know what you want to say and you know which medium you like best. However, it is not as important that your message be clear to you as it is that it be clear to the person you want to receive your message. It is less important how you like to send a message than how others like to receive messages.

    Basically, this idea is taken from marketing. It means that you must package your ideas in ways that make it easy for others to tune in to your ideas. This does not mean that you have to change your ideas, simply their presentation.

    An example from the advertising world will make this point clear. A television commercial for a toothpaste presents two attractive people of the opposite sex. What is the advertiser trying to sell you? Toothpaste, fewer cavities, or better interpersonal relations?

What the advertiser is telling you is that you too will have greater sex appeal if you use this particular brand. And the young adult market hears the message loud and clear.

But what if the intended audience is children? Do the advertisers use the same sex appeal approach: "Use your toothpaste and be the sexiest 5-year-old on the block"? Of course not. They focus on the good flavor and the prevention of cavities. Why? Because the audience is really the parents of 5-year-olds. But the contents of the two brands are almost identical. They are just packaged and marketed differently in order to "appeal to others where they are." It works. Try it and you will see. But remember that it all starts with being sensitive to the needs of the person on the receiving end of your message.

> *Build your message backwards from where others are,*
> *not where you want them to be or where you are.*

2. **Strive to help the receiver know why your message is important.** As we noted in discussing the differences in team members in Rule Five, people perceive the world around them in their own terms. Their terms and your terms may not be the same. Therefore, you need to understand the interests and needs of the people with whom you are communicating. The best way to get their attention is through what marketers call "benefits selling." Consider the following example.

Burt Hinson is a very successful salesperson for a large insurance company. He has made contact with a potential new client, Jim Steward. They are meeting at Jim's house tonight to discuss Jim's insurance program. After a brief casual conversation, Burt gets to the point.

"Jim, let me ask you a few questions."

"All right," says Jim.

"Jim, do you have all the money that you really need in your life?"

"No, of course not," responds Jim.

"OK," says Burt. "Let me ask you another question. If you were to die tomorrow, would your family have enough money for the mortgage, for living expenses, for college for your lovely kids?"

Jim hesitates, and Burt quickly holds up his hand and says, "That's OK, Jim, I understand. But let me ask you just one more question, Jim. Do you love your family?"

Gulp! Now Jim has a problem he did not have a few minutes ago. He is motivated to listen to Burt as they discuss ways to close the gap between Jim's love for his family and his ability to provide security for them. Burt, of course, is in a position to "help Jim solve *his* problem."

Of course, this example is a little extreme, but it makes the point. You have probably had something not too different from this happen to you. Burt has told Jim "why he should listen" and has "made it clear how Burt's message can help Jim."

Now link this idea to your projects. When you want someone to focus on your idea, think first what that person's piece of the project is. What is the person's objective that ties to the overall project goal? And perhaps more to the point, what task is the person focused on right now that ties to his objective, which in turn ties to the overall project goal? Use the Schedule charts (updated to the present) that we discussed with Rule Four to know what each team member is currently working to accomplish. Know what issues or concerns each is facing. Then design your message in this context. Using this knowledge can be the most powerful means for getting your message across.

3. **Keep others on the project team and stakeholders regularly informed.** You can be a better communicator if you regularly keep information flowing. Today's information technology options make regular communications so much easier than in the past. Communicate both formally (e.g., project review meetings, regular electronic reports) and informally (e.g., quick e-mails, voicemails, and hall meetings). One of the biggest mistakes many project managers make is not communicating with team members in a consistent, ongoing fashion. Furthermore, they do not communicate regularly with key stakeholders (e.g., clients, end users, and upper management) and then seem surprised when interested parties "blow the project plan out of the water."

No one on a project really likes surprises, especially negative ones. So keep everyone posted regularly!

Regular use of the project schedule and information from team members allows you to monitor progress along the project's course. Such information sharing is the key to avoiding many communication problems and is essential to empowering team members to fix problems when they do occur. Likewise, keeping your clients, end users, and other stakeholders informed and updated helps minimize the likelihood of having the rug pulled out from under you at the eleventh hour. By not surprising top management, you will find that your requests to them will tend to be of a smaller incremental nature. And small incremental requests have a higher probability of being granted than huge resource requests to solve big problems. Plus, unwelcome delays will be reduced significantly, which keeps everyone excited by the project.

4. **Communicate assertively and with understanding.** Do you communicate assertively, or aggressively? Perhaps you tend to be submissive. What difference does it make? And don't information technology mechanisms really take out all that emotional aspect of communicating anyway? Well, emotions make a lot of difference, and no, emotions do not go away with technology. In fact, technology can make this emotional aspect of communication much worse, because emotions are harder to convey in e-mails, text messages, and so forth than in face-to-face talks.

   Many people do not understand the difference between being assertive and being aggressive. They think that communicating assertively means making sure that they get their point across and have it acted on. But that kind of communication is really aggressive. This blindness to the difference becomes readily apparent when people send messages in one-way electronic messages through e-mail or voicemail. The focus is only on getting your point across, hence you can come across as aggressive.

   Figure 7.2 illustrates the difference between assertive, aggressive, and submissive communications. When you are aggressive, you promote only your ideas and try to exclude the ideas of others. If you have the bigger club, you will probably win, at least in the short run. When you are submissive, your ideas are the ones that get lost. The ideas of others will be adopted, assuming that others are not also submissive. When you are assertive, you try to be sure that your ideas are heard, but you also try to listen to the other per-

	Your ideas	Other's ideas
Aggressive	Used	Lost
Assertive	Heard	Heard
Submissive	Lost	Used

Figure 7.2 Framework for Understanding Aggressive, Assertive, and Submissive Communications

son's ideas. The result is true communication and better problem solving because both people get their ideas out on the table and attended to.

Let's look at an example. Suppose a member of your project team calls and leaves you a voicemail that loudly says: "I've got a great idea how to handle this problem we've been having. Just listen. We can fire the subcontractor and redo their work ourselves by working overtime." And this person goes on and on for several minutes, then stops talking and ends by saying, "OK?" Was this person assertive or aggressive? Most of us would say aggressive, because it was all one-way communication and the individual did not make any effort to draw out your ideas or solicit your input. Even the "OK?" at the end was more a statement than a question.

Contrast that scene with the following scenario of the same situation. The person comes to your office and says, "I've got an idea how we could solve the problem we've been having. Let me tell you about it, and then get your reactions and ideas, too. I think we should consider firing the subcontractor and redoing the work ourselves by working overtime. What do you think?" A two-way conversation follows with a final decision to first talk with the subcontractor one more time to see if the work can be corrected. Most people would say this was the assertive version because both parties' ideas were stated and considered and a shared decision was made in a face-to-face meeting. Did it have to be face-to-face? No, but it needed to be a two-way dialogue, even if it was in a series of back and forth e-mail messages. The key was the intent and the focus on information moving in two directions.

When two people communicate assertively, four outcomes are possible:

1.   Your idea is used.

2.   The other person's idea is used.

3.   A compromise of ideas is used.

4.   The really exciting possibility—a completely new set of ideas that neither of you had thought of—emerges and is used. Two heads really are better than one.

The key to assertive communication, and the distinction in the above two scenarios, is the concept of understanding. Being understanding means that you actively focus on making sense of the other person's ideas. If the person is quiet and does not volunteer thoughts, your focus should be on drawing out their original ideas and reactions to your ideas. If the person is submissive, your focus will need to be almost entirely on understanding and very little on assertiveness. If the person is aggressive, your focus may shift more toward assertiveness, although understanding can also help calm down the other person. When two people communicate assertively, they tend to use a relatively equal blend of assertiveness and understanding. The primary point is that by blending assertiveness and understanding, you will be focusing on the message going from sender to receiver and on the feedback going from receiver to sender. This can only improve the level of communication (and problem solving) on a project team.

One final note we should consider before we turn to the receiver side of communications. As the example above suggests, you need to think about the medium that will best serve the purpose of your message and the style of your intended receiver. E-mail, faxes, and voicemail may be efficient means of sending your message, but all can easily become one-way approaches that lose meaning for both you and the recipient. Often, the nature of your message and getting it across most clearly will call for two-way communication methods, such as telephone, face-to-face meetings, and team meetings. Sometimes you will need to be rather formal in holding a meeting with the team or filing a progress report with the client; other times it will be best to be informal and spontaneous. The point is to think about the nature of your message (e.g., its complexity and purpose) and how your intended recipient will best receive the message so that you achieve clarity and acceptance.

Listening for Impact

An often-overlooked aspect of leading projects to success is the power of listening. To really have significant impact on your project team, your clients, and all stakeholders, you need to be an effective listener. Unfortunately, most project leaders fail to exhibit good listening skills. Yet nearly half of the time spent in managing projects is focused on *receiving* information.

The core of the problem lies in the fact that we devote too little time to developing our listening skills. Most people tend to think of themselves as good listeners, but tests of listening comprehension show that we typically hear only about one quarter of the information that comes in our direction. We let the barriers to communication and the intense focus on our own ideas and needs muffle our listening abilities. But with a little discipline, you can become a much better listener. Below we offer eight suggestions that can help.

1. **Prepare yourself to listen.** To hear what another person is trying to tell you, you must want to hear the message coming to you. You need to scan constantly for messages of all types. Sometimes they come very directly and clearly; at other times they are almost imperceptible. Sometimes they will be verbal, sometimes in writing, and sometimes nonverbal. Being prepared means cutting down on the distractions (e.g., phone calls during a meeting in your office or checking e-mail while talking on the phone).

2. **Stop talking.** It is simply amazing how many project leaders seem to think that things get done faster if they talk more and listen less. What about you? Do you talk more than you listen? If so, you are probably less effective as a project leader than you could be (or think you are). Research shows that the best project leaders learn as much as possible about what is going on by listening carefully to others. When you stop talking you create the opportunity for others to communicate their ideas and concerns. You open up the chance for others to be empowered to use their talents and motiva-

tion. Stimulating others to talk is usually more important than listening to yourself talk, at least it is if you are interested in learning and using the best ideas! Or, as they say in the most successful and innovative project teams:

"No good idea ever entered the head through an open mouth."

3. **Listen with understanding.** Imagine yourself in the other person's position so that you can better appreciate the language and focus of the message. If the message is unclear, you need to use your combined understanding and assertive approach to clarify the message. Ask questions. Test to see if you really understand. If a team member is very angry, you may need to hear and acknowledge the anger before you can get to the real message. Let the other person know that you hear their anger and frustration. Remember, your primary objective when listening is to understand clearly the message being sent, both the literal message and the emotional message.

4. **Hear the speaker out completely.** Be sure you have heard the other person completely before you begin sending messages back. This does not mean that you cannot ask questions to clarify the message or paraphrase the message to check your interpretation. But be sure you do not cut off the person talking. Have you ever had someone complete a sentence for you? More often than not, people complete it incorrectly. Isn't this annoying? Then you must erase their misunderstanding and try again to get your idea through accurately.

*Your objective when listening is to understand
the message being sent.*

5. **Listen for what is *not* said.** Consider this example: you say to a team member, "Sharon, would you please check the files on the shelf-life studies and summarize the results in a memo by this Friday?" Sharon responds, "Sure, I'll look into it." Sound OK? You could easily assume that Sharon will get the job done by Friday. But wait a minute. What did Sharon not say? She did not say that she would prepare the memo and she did not say she would do it by Friday. A little more time on the issue and checking to ensure

clear communication might help avoid a disappointment for both of you on Friday.

6. **Listen for *how* something is said (the nonverbals).** Pay attention to the feelings or emotional level of the message. Notice eye contact, gestures, body language, tone of voice, timing, and other nonverbal signals. Over 70 percent of our interpersonal communication is nonverbal; only 30 percent of the message is in the words we use. Imagine trying to convince Noah that some part of the ark might need to be redesigned. What he says is, "I'm open to discussing it." What you "see," however, is how he remains behind his desk, sits back in his chair, crosses his arms, sticks his jaw out, and glares at you. Listening in this way suggests that Noah may not be all that "open" and may likely require a very persuasive argument!

   Or imagine a team meeting where two of the members have positioned themselves out of the circle. Two other people seem to be surveying the floor and the ceiling with their eyes. Only you and one other team member seem to be discussing working late on New Year's Eve. What do you think is going to happen when it comes time to work late on December 31? The nonverbal messages suggest that you may encounter some problems.

   Think about what happens to the nonverbals when you use e-mail to communicate. They are gone! And if 70 percent of the communication is gone, it is not hard to imagine that the potential for misunderstanding increases significantly. Even when we communicate over the telephone or through voicemail, most of the nonverbals are missing, again complicating successful listening. If you are in doubt about what you have heard, check it out before you draw a conclusion, and especially before you take action.

7. **Wait out pauses.** Give the team member who has an idea the time to share it with you fully. Wait for that department manager to collect her thoughts before she responds to your request for three of her people to work a greater percentage of their time on your project. You want people's true response, so be patient. When you are silent ("stop talking"), you invite others to fill the air with the sound of their voice. You also allow others to complete their thoughts in a way that will help you understand. Waiting out pauses allows pressure to drop and clarity to go up.

*Patience is a virtue that encourages
others to voice their thoughts.*

8. **Provide feedback.** Last, test for clarity and accuracy of what you
    are hearing. Let others know what you have heard and what you
    are going to do with their request, order, or information. Your first
    responsibility as a listener is to understand the message being sent
    to you. The second responsibility is to let the person know you
    understood the message accurately. Until this loop is completed,
    communication has not succeeded; only one-way transmission
    has occurred. The message must be sent from the sender to the
    receiver, and confirmation must go back to the sender from the
    receiver. Then you have two-way communication. When both par-
    ties are satisfied they have been heard accurately, communication
    has occurred.

If you are having trouble with communication on one of your projects, try instituting the "say-back technique." It works like this: John, one
of your team members, says something to you. Before you can say what
you want to say, you must paraphrase back to John in your own words
what he has said to you so he can decide if you received his message
accurately. If he is not satisfied, he must send it again, and you must say
it back again. This goes on until he is satisfied. Then you make your point,
and he must say it back to you until you are satisfied.

If you are having communication problems, this simple technique
will bring them to the surface. People are often appalled at how little they
have been hearing and at how hard it is to get points across among team
members so that everyone is satisfied with the process. The say-back
technique subtly begins making you and your project team members better listeners and better senders of messages. And that is the name of the
game in communication. Try it out; it works!

We can summarize the key points in this **DRIVER** rule by noting that
there is no trick to keeping people informed. It just takes discipline and
application of ideas we already know at some level. Effective communication is the key that unlocks the passageway from your head to others
and back again. The things you can do to get your message across and the
things you can do to make sure you hear what others are saying are not
complex, dramatic, or necessarily difficult. Anyone can do them. You
don't have to wait for someone else to do anything differently. Working

hard at sending your ideas more effectively and at being a better listener will not only make you a better communicator but will also improve the communication skills of others on your project team. Effective communication is contagious and a great disease for a project team to contract if you want a winning project.

Summary

Rule Seven:
Inform Everyone Regularly

1. Communications on projects fail because of many obstacles. Key ones include personal barriers between individuals, but more importantly, organizational blocks brought on by the very nature of projects.

2. Improving information flows, even in a world of amazing technological tools returns you to the basics of communication: namely, how you send your message and how well you listen to others.

3. To get your message across more effectively: (1) craft the message to address others where they are, (2) help others understand why your message is important to them, (3) connect everyone to the project by regular postings, and (4) communicate assertively and with understanding.

4. Effective listening is even more important than talking. Critical steps in listening include: (1) really wanting to hear the message, (2) listening without talking, (3) listening with understanding, (4) hearing the speaker out, (5) listening for what is *not* said, (6) paying attention to nonverbal signals, (7) waiting out pauses of the sender, and (8) providing feedback to check your understanding.

```
G               Develop an Empowered Project Team
  O               Reinforce Motivation and Energy
    C               Inform Everyone Regularly
      A               V
        R               E
          T               R
            S
```

Rule Eight: Vitalize People with Energy from Conflicts

Conflict creates energy that can vitalize everyone
on the team for positive payoff!

Conflict, oh no! Can't we just figure out a way to avoid conflict on our projects? The answer is, no. And even if you could eliminate it, you wouldn't want to. People do not have conflict over things they do not care about. So with conflict comes energy and passion. An effective project leader directs that energy in a way that can **V**italize people (the "**V**" in **DRIVER**) to get the job done—that is, to steer your **GOCART-S** across the finish line as a winner.

While you may have carefully planned and developed your **GOCART-S** for the race, once the race starts unforeseen events are likely to arise. Projects are just unpredictable. Moreover, obstacles along the route will become apparent only when you reach them. How to deal with these changes in your plan is likely to create disagreements among people. Coordinating and integrating the work of different people, many of whom do not report directly to you, also raises potential conflicts.

Indeed, conflicts are unavoidable in managing projects. Studies show that project leaders spend nearly half their time managing differences between team members. But the existence of disagreements and conflicts in a project is not only unavoidable, it is actually quite desirable. If managed properly, the energy from conflicts can ensure continued interest and commitment, encourage novel and integrative solutions, and spotlight potential inhibitors to arriving at the checkered flag.

Inherently, conflict is neither good nor bad; rather, it is the outcome of conflict that can be good or bad, functional or harmful, positive or negative. Marriage and family counselors often find couples divorcing because there is no conflict between the partners. Instead, they take each other for granted. The same thing can happen on your project team. Let's turn our focus to the types of conflicts that are typical in projects, then to understanding why these conflicts occur, and finally to learning how to direct the energy from conflicts in a positive direction.

Conflict is a source of energy to be embraced
and managed, not avoided or eliminated.

Types of Conflicts in Projects

Many types of conflicts derive directly from the inherent nature of projects, not from the people involved. By assigning blame for conflict to various people involved in the project, you push the energy in a negative direction. By understanding that people in conflict are the potential means for positive outcomes, you begin to develop the mindset needed to vitalize people from conflicts.

Conflicts occur for a variety of reasons. Project leaders report that conflicts typically arise over the following seven points of contention. Note that the first six are related more to the situation than to the people in the situation. People are not the source of conflict; they are the players in the situation. Indeed, they are the means for turning conflict into positive energy. Conflicts stem from these seven sources:

1. **Priorities of tasks and objectives.** Participants often have different views about the proper sequence of tasks and about the importance of tasks and objectives. Such differences occur not only

within the project team but also between the project team and other support groups, as well as between the team and the client.

2. **Administrative procedures.** Disagreements often arise over how a project will be managed—for example, over the definition of the project leader's reporting relationships and responsibilities, operational requirements, interdepartmental work agreements, and levels of administrative support.

3. **Technical opinions.** The less routine a project, the more likely it is that there are differences of opinion about the "best way" to accomplish the task. Disagreements may arise over specifications, technical trade-offs, and techniques to achieve the required performance. For example, the director and the film editor on a movie project may have entirely different and competing viewpoints on how best to achieve a certain effect with the camera and special effects.

4. **Staffing and resource allocations.** Conflicts arise over how best to allocate people to various projects and within project assignments. One team member complains that she always gets the "grunt work" while others get the glamorous assignments. Not only do individuals disagree over which projects their functional manager should assign them to, but they also face competing demands from their project leader and functional manager. This leads to both interpersonal strife and personal stress.

5. **Costs and budgets.** "How much is this going to cost?" and "Why is this costing so much?" are frequent sources of disagreement throughout a project. These differences often arise because it is difficult to estimate costs in the face of uncertainty. A functional support group, for example, may see the funds allocated by the project leader as insufficient for the work requested, while the client may feel that costs are too high.

6. **Schedules.** A constant source of tension is the client asking "How long is this going to take?" while the project team feels "I don't have enough time allocated to do a quality job." The tension really arises because we are dealing with estimates about the future, and the future can seldom be predicted with certainty. At the other extreme, if in making our estimates we take into account all the

possible things that could happen, the project might never be completed. Further, tension is often generated around the sequencing of events, as in the case of "Finish the documentation on this project before starting to program the next portion of the new accounting system."

7. **Interpersonal and personality clashes.** Conflicts arise not just over technical issues but also over "style" or "ego centered" issues like status, power, control, self-esteem, and friendships. Such conflicts may emerge from real personality and style differences, but often they are based on differences that emerge from departmental or organizational factors like varying past experience and different perspectives on time horizons.

Encountering Conflicts over the Life of a Project

Our studies, as well as those of numerous other researchers, reveal that the intensity of conflict for each of these sources varies over the life cycle of a project. While interpersonal and personality issues can occur at any time, the other six sources, which are often the real source of a conflict, occur at different and predictable times during the project. By taking note of when disagreements are likely to arise, you will be in a better position to manage them most effectively, thus creating positive energy from the conflicts.

During the **GOCART-S** *planning phase*, most conflicts arise over priorities, technical opinions, schedules, and costs. One reason that these four issues create so much turmoil is that project managers have limited control over other areas of the organization, particularly the functional support departments. That is why it is so helpful to involve as many people as possible in developing the **GOCART-S**. Get everyone on board early for a smoother race to the checkered flag.

As a project enters the *beginning of the implementation phase*, conflicts arise primarily over scheduling, priorities, staffing, administrative procedures, and technical issues. It is critical that you provide feedback on how the project is progressing and celebrate early accomplishments (marked by checkpoints). Frequent meetings and status review sessions help to develop interpersonal relationships that may be called upon in later, more stressful, stages of the project.

*Conflicts occur for different reasons and at
different points in the life of a project.*

As the project moves into *full-scale implementation* with full application of project resources, most conflicts will arise over scheduling issues and administrative procedures, especially when some tasks on the project's critical path fall behind schedule. Resolving these conflicts requires continual efforts to keep people focused on the project goal, posted on what everyone is doing, and updated on work in progress. Be certain that you update and revise schedule documents and distribute them to all affected parties.

As the team approaches the end of the project, *the finish line*, you will find conflicts developing over staffing, costs, and schedules. It is important to avoid losing the energy of key team members at this point in the project and to keep team members focused on the project goal all the way to the finish line. If they feel a sense of ownership in the project, they will more naturally identify with the project's final success and contribute to it through to completion.

Causes of Conflict in Projects

While it is helpful to think about the types of conflicts that can occur on a project and when in the project life cycle to expect them, it is even more helpful to reflect on the underlying causes of conflict on projects. If you are to determine effective ways to vitalize people in positive directions with the energy from conflicts, you must help everyone on the team understand these causes. The key reason is that conflicts do not occur between individuals, they arise between the roles people play in the project.

As we look briefly at the causes of conflict, take note that five of the six are determined almost directly from the nature of projects and the fact that projects are an overlay on the organizational processes. This point is important to acknowledge, because it means that the people in conflict can step back and focus on how they must work within and through the causes together to get to a place of positive energy. Let us briefly explore these six causes.

1. **Task interdependence.** People on a project team are brought into conflict because their work is so interdependent in nature. Each member's work means nothing by itself; rather, meaning comes

from the set of all tasks as a whole. As we discussed in Rule Two
on objectives, how people work to accomplish their objectives can
sometimes inhibit the work of others toward their objectives.
Since conflict can be defined as a blockage of achieving one's
objective, conflict grows directly from this unintended, but interdependent, blockage.

2. **Differing team member perspectives.** Because team members
come from different parts of the organization or even from different organizations, they bring different perspectives. Some may
respond to an urgency of time, while others are more focused on
quality, and others on cost control. Yet they must work together
and find a way to satisfy the perspectives of everyone. It can seem
as if people are on totally different pages or speaking different languages, and such differences can often lead to conflict.

3. **Ambiguous authority and responsibility.** In spite of significant
effort in developing your **GOCART-S**, you will always find some
ambiguity remaining in a project. With people separated by departmental or other such lines, this ambiguity can lead to tasks over-
lapping or to work falling between the cracks. Either result will
lead to disappointment and to potential conflict, as people naturally try to place blame for problems on specific individuals.

4. **Limited, common resources.** Have you ever worked on a project
that had enough resources? Such projects do not seem to exist. And
when people have to "fight" for the resources they need in a negotiation, they tend to adopt a "how do we divide up the pie" mentality, and conflict is almost inevitable. Team members tend to see
their own needs as most important. They think that without the
resources they need, they will not be able to complete their part of
the project. Hence, each person perceives a necessity to fight for
resources, with a resulting sense of conflict.

5. **Organizationally focused reward systems.** As we noted in Rule
Two when discussing objectives, few organizations are set up to
support the collaborative work needed on a project. Rewards, both
financial and nonfinancial, are almost never located within the
project team. They are in departments, divisions, or other such
business units. Hence, team members are drawn to satisfy unit
demands rather than project demands, thus leading to potential
conflicts that stem from rewards based on nonproject priorities.

6. **Personal skills and traits.** The last, and in many ways minor, cause of conflicts is the individual skills and traits that people on the team possess. While it is easy to think of everyone else as greedy and self-centered, it is just not true that these traits are so strong in team members as to be a major source of conflict. More important is that people often do not possess the skills needed to deal effectively with conflict. They can be reduced to self-interest because they lack conflict-resolution skills.

Building Agreements that Vitalize

Whatever the types or causes of conflicts that you encounter on a project, it is critical to know how to turn that energy into a positive force for the project. Conflicts cannot be avoided. The very nature of projects pushes people into conflict situations. So, when conflicts arise, you must be prepared to deal with them.

Focusing first on the six causes, a good starting point is to turn them around by employing a general attitude of rising above the causes to create positive energy from the conflicts. Consider the follow as options.

Turn:

1. *Task interdependence* into *Us against the problem.*

2. *Different perspectives* into *A shared vision.*

3. *Ambiguous roles* into *Ongoing dialogue about tasks.*

4. *Limited resources* into *Best use of what we have.*

5. *Organization rewards* into *Praise for team efforts.*

6. *Personal skills/traits* into *Conflict skills.*

These ideas are a great way to build the positive attitude that is essential for effective management of project conflict. But it takes more than a positive attitude to vitalize people from conflict. When you start to consider what actions to take, remember that as a project leader you cannot demand conflict resolution. You do not have the authority or position power for that approach to work, nor can you dictate attitude change. Instead, four tactics can help you build agreements that mobilize the energy from conflicts in a positive way:

1. Create a common ground.

2. Enlarge areas of agreement.

3. Gather information.

4. Focus on issues, not personalities.

1. **Create a common ground.** The most important step in building agreements is to form a strong foundation between the parties involved. Ask: "What do you and the other person already have in common? What do the two of you agree on? What are you both trying to accomplish?" Ideally, the goal of the project should sum up the common ground.

To mobilize positive energy, focus on what you have in common with the other party, not what you and the other person disagree on. Pushing people apart at the start of a dialogue seldom engenders an atmosphere of cooperation. In agreeing on a common ground, people highlight their necessary interdependencies. When my success is a function of your success, and vice versa, we are both more likely to listen and work through our differences than when our successes are viewed as independent of one another. This is, of course, one of the reasons why you must work diligently at the start of a project to involve all team members and stakeholders in determining the project's goal and creating a schedule that clarifies and underscores the interdependencies.

Competing points of view cannot be resolved by logic alone. Find a common ground from which to build agreement and redirect energy.

2. **Enlarge areas of agreement.** The second step is to build on these areas of agreement. This involves moving out of the "selling your idea" or "if I can only convince them!" mode of thinking. The key to the transition from debating to building is an exchange of statements. Instead of allowing point and counterpoint debates, set an example by making and encouraging the other person to make statements like "If you would be willing to do X, then I would be willing to do Y." Or "Let's consider this option that might satisfy both of our needs." This kind of exchange can be very hard to set

up because our egos deeply entrench us in our positions. That is why you must let go of positions in the first place and find the project's common ground that can guide the negotiation.

A certain amount of time is needed to allow people to get their ideas out on the table. Too often, however, participants in a conflict continue attacking and defending and devote little time to building an agreement. The building process is facilitated when you (1) allow each person to state his or her position without interruption, (2) allow a brief period of time for questions of clarification only, and (3) ask the question "How can each of us get what we want?" When arguing is leading nowhere, the skilled negotiator switches to statements of possible exchange. Try asking "What is each of you willing to give in on in order to get something back?" This question can transform the argument into a discussion and the potential deadlock into a settlement.

3. **Gather information.** An important problem-solving technique in managing conflicts is to gather information before jumping to a position. Working through fundamental issues, such as "Who is in conflict?", "Who can resolve the conflict?", and "Is all the information available?" helps to create a working foundation for dialogue. If you cannot agree which parties are really involved in the conflict, some important points of view may not be represented in the negotiations. The needs of these people will in turn not be represented in the proposed solutions.

    Likewise, too often you can be arguing over a problem the other person cannot resolve. Disagreements about "what should have happened" often fall into this category. Discussing who should be involved in the negotiation is one way of determining what types of information are needed to build an agreement. This technique forces you to consider "Who will be affected by this agreement?" Research clearly shows that people are most likely to follow through on an agreement that they have helped shape.

4. **Focus on issues, not personalities.** Finally, it is crucial to depersonalize the conflict. When you feel that you have to defend yourself from personal attack, your response typically takes one of two forms. Either you fight back, which only escalates the disagreement and makes the possibility of finding common ground negligible, or you flee. In the latter case, you don't encourage people to

commit their energies to problem solving. Although they may agree to an action, they will have no real commitment to follow through once you are out of sight. And in a fight, the other person's energies are devoted to getting back at you and not to solving the problem.

One of the best ways to focus on issues and not personalities is to be future oriented: "What are we going to do about this?" rather than "Why can't you be more responsible?" or "Who got us into this situation?" By being future oriented, you emphasize building agreement on a future course of action rather than blaming each other for past problems. This is not to say that you don't want to explore the past for insight into the causes of problems, but emphasizing the past often leads to one person having to defend his or her actions or to blame and scapegoat someone else. "What are we going to do to ensure that this doesn't happen again?" is a statement of allies against the problem instead of enemies against each another.

Successful Negotiators of Conflict

It is clear from the preceding discussion that successful project leaders are effective negotiators in managing differences. Much has been written about how successful negotiators behave, both what they do and what they avoid doing, as they build agreements between people with differences. Often, technically skilled project leaders discover that they rely too heavily on reasoning and logic in trying to get others to do what they want them to do.

The objective of negotiation is to reach an agreement that satisfies both parties. Satisfaction is an emotional, not a logical, experience. Negotiation is not an optimal, dispassionate problem-solving experience. It is more emotional than rational. For example, how could Noah have proved that it would rain for 40 days and 40 nights or whether such a storm really would flood the earth?

The best solution in negotiations is one that makes all parties feel like winners and results in committed follow-through on the solution. This does not suggest that analytical skills are not needed in negotiation, just that they are not paramount. They take up time and may get in the way of efforts that could be devoted to building an agreement.

Analytical skills may actually get in the way of resolving conflicts.

Since good project leaders must be skillful negotiators in order to turn conflicts into positive energy for the project, each of the following nine techniques needs to be part of your repertoire:

1. **Be direct but not offensive.** Act to find solutions rather than react to problems. Be a problem finder. Be clear about your interests and about your needs.

2. **Preface your statements.** For clarity and to reduce ambiguity about your intentions, preface negotiation points with remarks such as: "What I'd like to do is propose . . . ." or "May I make this suggestion . . . ."

3. **Avoid argument.** Argument during the negotiation dilutes the process and gets people off the track of searching for and building upon agreements. Remember, arguments are emotional.

4. **Be aware of the limitations of logic.** Rather than rely too heavily on logic and reason, try the following attitude: "What seems reasonable to you is reasonable to me." Exchange statements play a pivotal role in this process. Sensitivity to others' perceptions is vital.

5. **Know what you want and ask for it.** If you don't know what you want, you can't ask for it. If you don't ask for it, you're not likely to get it. Nobody can read your mind, nor can you read anyone else's mind. Assertive expressions of needs, interests, and possible exchanges help move the negotiations along.

6. **Repeat expectations firmly.** Persist in stating expectations, wants, and needs and in not letting the other person off too easily or making it easy to say no. By building on common ground, make it possible for the other person to say yes.

7. **Don't justify.** Too often, justification seems like rationalization and clutching at straws. Rather than justify defensively, make firm assertions backed by facts when appropriate.

8. **Avoid "irritants."** Certain words and phrases are irritants, like: "Anyone could see that." Or "It's always been done this way." Or "My generous offer is . . . ." Such comments push the other party

into a corner where the only option is to fight or flee. Keep the discussion focused on the issues and not on personalities.

9. **Create alternative solutions.** Understand that both your own interests and those of others can probably be satisfied by more than one solution. Imagination is required both to understand what the other person wants or needs and to search for solutions to satisfy those needs and yours. Often this entails numerous "What if?" statements. Don't be afraid to send up trial balloons for possible agreement.

By effectively managing and negotiating conflicts, you achieve positive outcomes from the inevitable differences that arise in moving your **GOCART-S** forward. You get the job done most effectively when you build agreements that vitalize all team members. Conflict creates energy that is essential for managing projects from inception to completion. Anticipating the sources of conflict and understanding the ebb and flow of conflicts in a project environment will increase your ability to harness this energy for positive impact on your project's success.

Summary

Rule Eight: Vitalize People with Energy from Conflicts

1. Learn to manage conflicts rather than avoid them if you want to be a winning project leader. Conflict represents an emotional commitment to a project, and when kept under control, it leads team members to solve problems cooperatively.

2. Different types of conflict arise over the life cycle of a project. By knowing when and why these conflicts can occur, you can effectively channel team members' energies.

3. Learn the causes of conflicts and help the team appreciate that the causes are more situationally based than based within the people. People are the means to resolution of the problem, not the cause of it.

4. Resolve conflicts by building a positive attitude and using four critical skills: (1) create a common ground, (2) enlarge areas of agreement, (3) gather information, and (4) focus on issues, not personalities.

5. Effectively negotiating conflict requires that all parties come away satisfied, not just rationally but emotionally. Learn the skills of successful negotiators of conflict.

G	**D**evelop an Empowered Project Team
O	**R**einforce Motivation and Energy
C	**I**nform Everyone Regularly
A	**V**italize with Energy from Conflicts
R	**E**
T	**R**
S	

Rule Nine: Empower Yourself and Others

To truly empower others, you must give power away.
But doing so actually increases your power!

Your project **GOCART** can't get across the finish line and merit the checkered flag without power to drive it forward. To achieve astonishing project results, you must learn to create a culture that empowers both yourself and others on the project team. In Rule Five, we focused on developing an empowered project team. Here we focus on creating a culture that will **E**mpower everyone involved with the project (the "**E**" in **DRIVER**).

Interestingly enough, everyone wants power, although many people feel power is somehow bad. Power in and of itself is not bad, and it is essential for achieving desired project results. Unless you can make people feel powerful on your project, you will not be able to tap into their full knowledge, experience, and internal motivation. Few people on project teams believe they have enough power. Haven't you heard these laments? "If I only had the authority necessary to get those people on track . . . ." "If only I had the power to influence my superiors . . . ." "What I need to

107

get this done is more authority . . . ." No matter what level of managers we have worked with, regardless of setting or function, all have thought that their impact on projects would be better if only they had more power.

Part of what limits us in our use of power for project results is that we tend to associate power with *position* in the organization. But this restricted view of power is detrimental to projects. Project leaders seldom have position power over everyone involved in the project. Effective project leaders understand that power is dynamic and like electricity, it is all around us, virtually infinite in its potential. Your challenge is to find ways to tap into this energy and to harness and channel its forces. Like money in the bank, power is a source of credit that expands with use and with proper use can also make other people feel stronger and more powerful.

Literally, the word power means "to be able." It is the capacity someone has to influence others, and it encompasses much more than one's position in an organization. Making something happen arises at least as much from personal competence as it does from resources associated with one's position. Indeed, project leaders, who almost always have limited position power, must draw upon personal sources of power if they are to succeed.

Personal power is a set of skills and abilities possessed by an individual. It refers to ways you work with and respond to others in various situations. Most important, it does not come from the organizational title you hold. It comes from within you and from the ways in which others perceive you. It travels with you as you move through the organization, influencing others to get the job done on the project.

Six Sources of Power

Power has been conceptualized as coming from one or more of six sources. The first three come from position, and are limited for project leaders, and the last three come from the individual and are virtually limitless. As we review these sources of power, think of which ones you have that you can use, and also think of the power sources that others on your project teams possess. By drawing on all the sources available to you and to others, you can empower everyone to achieve some astonishing results on your projects.

Position Sources of Power

1. **Reward power** is based on the perception that another person can reward or grant resources that others desire. The person who controls your paycheck has reward power over you.

2. **Coercive power** is based on the perception that another person can punish or withhold valued resources from us. For example, the person who can fire you has coercive power over you.

3. **Legitimate power** is based on the internalized belief that another person has the legitimate right to request certain types of actions and that you have a social obligation to comply with the request. The person who has a bigger title than you has legitimate power over you.

Personal Sources of Power

4. **Referent power** is based on a desire to identify with another person and the belief that going along with that person's requests will facilitate a favorable interpersonal relationship and will foster mutual respect. When you respect and admire someone for a particular talent, that person has power over you. Why do you think professional athletes are used in ads to sell products?

5. **Expert power** is based on a perception that another person has special knowledge, skill, or information relevant to the task or problem at hand. If you work around computers and someone you work with knows computers in depth, that person's opinion will carry more weight than yours might; thus, that person has expert power over you.

6. **Relationship power** is based on a feeling that a caring work relationship or friendship exists between you and another person. If a friend asks you for a favor, you are more likely to say yes than if a stranger asks; hence your friend has relationship power over you (though it may be reciprocal in this case).

As a project leader, you face real limits to the amount of position power you have. And even if you have vast amounts of position power, you are limited as to the amount that you can and should use. For example, how many times can you fire someone? How often can you give someone a raise or promotion? By contrast, there is virtually no limit to the amount of personal power you may possess, and you can use this power much more freely. In fact, you can use personal power to help draw out the power that lies in others on the project team, which is the real focus of empowering others.

Power and Performance

How does it happen that one branch, department, or unit of a company is more effective than another similar group working under identical company policies, procedures, and organizational structures? Researchers into this phenomenon identify power and its distribution as a key factor in effectiveness. A consistent finding is that managers in the underachieving units hoard power. In the high-performing units, the managers share power.

Consequently, people at every level in the high-performing units feel that they can, and should, be responsible for their unit's effectiveness. Contemporary management thought holds that it is powerlessness that corrupts rather than excessive power. When you empower people on your project team, you create in them a real sense of responsibility and involvement. Empowered people feel that they have and can use power to help achieve the project goal. Studies have shown that when people feel they have power, they can and do make a difference. Projects get done on time, within budget, and with high quality.

Other studies of effective project leaders have reported significant relationships between performance and the use of various power bases. For example, the less team members perceive that project leaders are using position power and the more they perceive that project leaders are using personal power, the greater are the levels of member involvement and openness of upward communication, and the higher is the productivity level of the team. Similar findings emerge from other studies involving such diverse occupations as sales personnel, college teachers, insurance underwriters, postal service carriers, and assembly-line workers.

Effective project leaders build and rely on personal sources of power to inspire others to get things done.

Using Power to Get the Results You Want

When you use power to influence others, you can expect people to respond in one of three different ways. They may demonstrate *commitment* to your request and enthusiastically engage in the desired behavior. Alternatively, they may *comply* and go along with your request because they feel they have to, but they probably do not do anything beyond what is minimally required. Or they may *resist* by failing to follow through or by fighting back. Obviously, you need to understand how the various power bases can be used to generate commitment or, at least, willing compliance rather than resistance to your requests. The key to eliciting commitment is in how you use personal power sources and in not using position power too much. If you make effective use of all the sources of power, you will be able to empower others to use their talents to get things done in ways that will truly amaze you.

Building and Using Referent Power. You develop referent power when others on the project respect and admire you personally. This source of power is determined by the way you treat people. For example, showing consideration for their needs and feelings, dealing with each person fairly, and standing up for the group are ways to increase referent power. Regular interaction with each individual on the team is essential.

Another way you create referent power is by setting a positive example. You should intentionally set an example of what you expect and want from others. In fact, you really can't ask anyone else to do something you would not be willing to do yourself, without being hypocritical.

Over the many years of his career at GE, Jack Welch touted the value of education. To back up his words, he regularly taught in the new managers program offered to all GE managers. As another example, if quality is important, make it the first item on every meeting's agenda and the first question you ask when reviewing the project's progress with individuals on the team. Whenever Noah met with God, what do you think they talked about first? A major reason for Noah's commitment to the ark project was his trust (faith) in God. God had referent power with Noah, and Noah probably used this same source of power to gain commitment from his team.

Building and Using Relationship Power. You develop relationship power by getting to know your team's members and by using the skill of listening (which we focused on with Rule Seven). As you get to know the team members, and just as important, as they get to know you, you develop a sense of relationship with each other. When things need to be done for the benefit of the project, this relationship power can be extremely useful.

The driving force behind developing these relationships has to be you, the project leader. If you risk letting people get to know you and you take an interest in them, a sense of family begins to develop. It is this sense of family that causes people to commit and want to put forth their best efforts on the project. One CEO we worked with really knew how to develop and use relationship power. By taking a genuine interest in his people and by letting them get to know him (even his love of playing the saxophone), he built relationships that yielded commitment from employees that is above and beyond the call.

Every day you develop relationship power as you listen attentively to project team members. What are their concerns, their personal goals? What is happening in their lives? Not that you should necessarily try to solve their personal problems, but the empathy that comes from listening lets them know you care. People generally go the extra mile for someone they know cares for them.

Building and Using Expert Power. You can't influence other people just because you're the technical expert. They must recognize that you are competent and perceive you to be a credible source of information and advice. Indeed, sharing the information you possess is one of the most effective ways to create a culture of empowerment. Furthermore, when you share your expertise by teaching others what you know, your expert power comes alive and provides others with the knowledge to positively impact the project. You cannot maintain a sense of expertise unless you keep up with the latest developments in your field and remain professionally active, but you must not hoard this knowledge. To maintain expert power, you have to share it with others as you continue to learn new things.

But keep in mind that expert power can be undermined by relying too heavily on logic and rational reasoning as persuasion tactics, especially if you come across as a "know it all." Be tactful. You will generally receive a negative reaction from people if you flaunt your expertise and experience. It is counterproductive to try to convince others by belittling their arguments or making them feel stupid. If you want people to feel empowered, you cannot do things to make them feel stupid. Don't treat the objections, concerns, or suggestions of others as unimportant, trivial, or insignificant. Recognize the contributions of others, respect their knowledge and experience, and incorporate, whenever possible, their ideas into action plans.

Besides, you may not always be the expert. It may be that others on the project team are the subject matter experts. Noah, for example, may not have been the expert on sails for the ark. By drawing upon the expertise of knowledgeable team members, Noah could ensure a better ark (project output) while also demonstrating his ability to know what "he did not know." You need to be sufficiently familiar with the work and capabilities of others. You need to work to understand their language and to respect their problems and viewpoints so you can coordinate and integrate their efforts and activities. In this way, you achieve expert power, even though, strictly speaking, you are not the expert. But more importantly, your perceived expert power is being used to empower others so that much more gets done more easily.

Project leaders develop and use personal power to empower
others and to achieve astonishing results.

Using Legitimate Power. It is important to know how to use whatever position power you have to create a culture of empowerment for others. You can exercise your authority by making a legitimate request—one that should come from the project leader. But you will encounter less resistance if you make it easy for others to go along with your request. One way to do this is to make "polite" requests. This is especially important for project personnel who are likely to be sensitive to status differences and to authority relationships (for example, someone older than you or someone with multiple supervisors). Polite requests generally use the word "please," even when you have legitimate power. Try it; it works.

Another way to make it easy for others to go along is to explain the reasons behind your request. People are more likely to go along with your requests when they see them as consistent with agreed-upon task objectives. Sometimes it is helpful to review the decision process you used to arrive at an action plan with the team. By taking them through the process step by step, you can help them see why the decision was made and why other alternatives were rejected. In fact, by having a clear project goal and objectives and plan (a well-designed **GOCART-S**), you can legitimize actions without having to be heavy-handed. In actuality, by defining clear boundaries of action, you create a sense of autonomy and responsibility in members of the project team.

Finally, it is helpful when project personnel understand that your requests are within the scope of your authority. Linking requests with official documentation such as written rules, policies, contract provisions, and schedules is one way to do this. You may not get away with just saying "trust me," unless people on the team perceive that a higher authority is on your side (as God was on Noah's side). Such clear boundaries allow people to take necessary action even before you say anything. Now that's effectively using legitimate power!

Using Reward Power. The most common way of using reward power is to offer tangible benefits to people if they go along with your requests. However, the ideal conditions for effectively using reward power seldom exist for project leaders, who typically lack control over attractive financial rewards. Furthermore, project team members often have interdependent tasks that make it less effective to offer individual incentives.

More importantly as related to developing a culture of empowerment, reward power may not be that effective in gaining a sense of commitment from the team. You may obtain compliance with rules and policies with the promise of rewards, but you are unlikely to obtain the person's heart or commitment. Gary Yukl in his book *Leadership in Organizations* points out these problems. When people perform tasks in order to obtain a promised reward, they perceive their behavior as a means to an end. This may tempt them to take shortcuts and neglect less visible aspects of the task in order to complete the assignment and obtain the reward. Internal incentives, which motivate a person to put forth extra effort beyond what is required, will be minimized if external rewards are overused. Rewards come to be expected every time something new or unusual is required. Most managers run out of tangible goodies, especially as expectations escalate. In addition, using reward power can lead to resistance and resentment because people feel you are manipulating them by the contingent ("If you will do this, I will do that") nature of the relationship.

Consequently, rather than using rewards as explicit incentives, you need to recognize and reinforce desired behavior more subtly. The key is to focus on rewarding intrinsic needs like recognition, self-esteem, and future opportunities for growth and challenge. Instead of financial rewards or formal recognition, focus more on the personal aspects of "praising" people for their work. When you give nonfinancial rewards in a way that expresses your personal appreciation for the efforts and accomplishments of each team member, you tend to get positive commitment from people. Interpersonal relationships are more satisfying when they are viewed as an expression of mutual friendship and loyalty rather than as an impersonal economic exchange.

Using Coercive Power. Effective project leaders avoid using coercive power except when absolutely necessary. It is likely to create resentment and erode their personal power base. With coercion there is little chance of gaining commitment. Even willing compliance is difficult to achieve.

Coercion is most appropriate when it is used to stop significant behaviors that are detrimental to project success (e.g., theft, sabotage, violation of safety rules, or insubordination). Strategies of "positive discipline," rather than scaring people with threats or sample doses of punishment, are directed toward inducing people to assume responsibility for helping resolve the discipline problem. Here are some guidelines for using positive discipline:

- Let people know about the rules and penalties for violations.
- Administer discipline consistently and promptly.
- Provide sufficient warning before resorting to punishment.
- Get the facts before reprimanding or punishing.
- Stay calm and avoid appearing hostile.
- Use punishments sparingly and only as appropriate to the situation.
- Administer warnings and punishments in private.

Effective project leaders know that having to use coercion means they have to some extent lost control of the project. Efforts to empower others are failing. Don't be too quick to punish team members. If the team is feeling empowered, they can bring people back into line far easier than you can.

Giving People What They Want (Need) from Their Leaders

It should be apparent that among these various sources of power, the reaction to power use is based in the "eye of the beholder": What counts is what others perceive. Still, the way you handle yourself, people's interactions with you, and your managerial style all influence the perception of your power and hence the effect you can have on people's behavior.

What exactly is it that others expect of you as the project leader? Actually, a lot, but a few things seem to be essential, especially if you want people to feel and act empowered. In our research, we have identified four personal characteristics that people admire, look for, and expect most from those whom they are willing to follow. As we describe these elements, think about how you measure up in the eyes of your project team members.

The most frequently mentioned characteristic is *honesty*. People want a leader who is truthful with them and who can be trusted. Unless people trust you, you will never get them to take the risks to act empowered. They will hear you say one thing but act another way, and this inconsistency will cause them to retreat from becoming responsible, empowered team members. People judge your honesty by observing your behavior. Do you do what you say you are going to do, or not?

Sam Walton, founder of Wal-Mart Stores once told his employees that if they achieved their profit objectives, he would put on a hula skirt and dance down Wall Street. They did. And he did! Being honest is, of course, a game involving risk. The leader must be the first one to ante up.

> *People want to feel that their leaders are honest,*
> *competent, forward-looking, and inspiring.*

Another highly desired characteristic in leaders is competence. Before they will follow a request from you, people must believe that you know what you are asking. This does not mean you have to know everything. Indeed, recognizing when someone on the team knows more than you do about a particular issue can actually enhance the perception of your competence. By acknowledging the competence in others, you also demonstrate your level of trust in others—not unlike the kind of trust you want others to feel toward you.

Having a *forward-looking sense of direction* is also critical for a leader. This trait should be a natural for project leaders. People who lead projects need to know where the project is going and to be concerned about the future of the project. By working hard to keep the project goal in the forefront of team members' minds, you instill a comfortable sense that the team and the project are headed in the right direction. You help the team feel the power to act with autonomy, since they can assess whether their actions will help move the project toward its goal. Your clarity about the target and the project objectives are akin to "magnetic north." With a compass you can more easily guide the team forward and keep it on course, and if everyone has a compass, everyone can contribute to keeping the project on course.

Finally, people expect leaders to be *inspiring*. It is important that you be seen as enthusiastic, energetic, and positive about the project. Being inspiring is not necessarily being an evangelist, but it is being willing to let others know what you care about. Max Dupree, former chairman of Herman Miller Furniture, would ask his senior executives: "What would make you weep with emotion? What would make you feel excited deep down inside?" To be inspiring you need to be able to express genuine excitement and emotion for the project vision and with the operating values that will guide people's work on the project.

As one very successful project leader told us, "I think most of us are looking for a calling, not a job. Most of us have jobs that are too small for our spirit." This statement is a reminder that you must help people find a greater sense of purpose and worth in their day-to-day work on the project. What is the passion in your project? Can you identify it and develop it in others?

> *You must help people find a sense of purpose and worth*
> *in their work if they are to feel empowered.*

What do these four central leadership attributes add up to? What does it mean to be honest? To be competent? To be forward-looking and inspirational? These characteristics are the essence of a leader's *credibility*. When you are perceived as trustworthy, as knowing what you are talking about, as dynamic and sincere, and as having a sense of direction, others will see you as credible. And when you have credibility, people are likely to comply with your requests and even more likely to demonstrate a sense of commitment in their follow-through regardless of the power source you use. Both you and others will feel empowered! And empowerment is the energy that allows you to use the full force of your **S**upercharged **GOCART**, as well as the power that lies within the members of your project team, to get your project to the finish line for the checkered flag.

Summary

Rule Nine:
Empower Yourself and Others

1. Power is what leaders use to enable themselves and others to get things done; it is the capacity for accomplishment.

2. Most of the true power that project leaders have comes not from position power but from personal power, which derives from three sources: referent, expert, and relationship power.

3. Effective project leaders use power to gain commitment from team members and to tap into the power of team members so that they become truly engaged in driving the project to the checkered flag.

4. Greater levels of project involvement and communication are found when leaders share power with team members.

5. People look for four personal characteristics in leaders: honesty, competence, a sense of direction, and inspiration. When these characteristics are found, leaders are perceived as credible and team members feel empowered to act.

G   Develop an Empowered Project Team
O   Reinforce Motivation and Energy
C   Inform Everyone Regularly
A   Vitalize with Energy from Conflicts
R   Empower Yourself and Others
T   R
S

Rule Ten: Risk Being Creative

Those who want everything to be right the first time will never take the risk of innovating.

Risk taking for the sake of creativity completes the **DRIVER** acronym (the final "**R**"). It is the final leader skill for successfully bringing your **GOCART-S** to the checkered flag. Without opportunities to be innovative and daring, you win few races and complete even fewer projects with quality, on time, and within budget. Risk taking is essential if you are to be creative, and projects without creativity seldom reach the finish line first.

And the wonderful truth is that creativity can be induced. You can "create" the creativity that can make your project a winner, by influencing many of the factors that have been identified as facilitating or hindering creative behavior. Innovative behavior in organizations is not simply a matter of selection, training, or good fortune. It is a matter of attitude and action. Mistakes must be acceptable on your projects. Encourage people to take thoughtful action and to learn from mistakes.

Let us explore this skill of promoting creativity and innovation on your projects. As a first step, let's consider the factors that keep people on project teams from being creative. Then we discuss ways to facilitate creativity and develop better ideas to solve problems your projects will inevitably encounter.

Blocks to Creativity

Creative behavior is the expression of creative ability, which everyone has to varying degrees. One reason for the absence of creative behavior on your projects may be that people on the team feel inhibited from expressing their talents. Anxiety, fear of evaluation, defensiveness, and cultural inhibition are all blocks to the realization of creative potential. Managerial practices and organizational policies that foster such negative reactions hinder the expression of creative talent.

Project leaders who stress the consequences of failure rather than rewards for success tend to inhibit the expression of new ideas. Conversely, a climate that supports risk taking adopts the attitude of Thomas Edison: "I failed my way to success." Tom Peters puts it this way: "Blow it up; go back to square one and reinvent."

Organizational instability can also inhibit creative expression. Unstable organizations are unpredictable to their members, and they breed insecurity and anxiety. But on projects, it is not productive to try to achieve stability through excessive formalization of rules, policies, relationships, and procedures. High levels of formalization interfere with interunit communications and discourage experimentation. Centralization of decision making in the project leader restricts the free exchange of information and slows communication. These delays tend to dampen enthusiasm, increase response times, and heighten the probability that information is lost or distorted. A highly centralized project structure can easily inhibit creativity and innovation and the empowered use of people's creative talents.

Leave time in your project for thinking, experimenting, and being creative. Sometimes it pays to adopt the attitude that says: "Don't just do something, sit there." The creative process takes time; how much time is not clear. When creativity is viewed as nonprogrammed activity, then the following statement comes into play: "Programmed work drives out nonprogrammed work." In such circumstances, the probability that project participants will make time for creative efforts is low. Innovative companies guard against this possibility by institutionalizing a "bootleg" process. Everyone is expected to spend 10–15 percent of their time working on nonprogrammed activities.

Don't just do something, sit there (and think)!

Facilitating Creativity and Innovation

Studies have identified several structural elements and practices that facilitate creative efforts: *reinforcement, goals, deadlines* (like milestones), and *freedom*. By developing policies and practices that encourage individual creativity, you can develop and maintain higher levels of innovation. Let's explore these ideas in more detail.

Creative behavior, like any other type of behavior, is influenced by its outcome. When you ignore or punish risk taking or when creative efforts are stifled, threatened, ridiculed, or stolen, creative energies are likely to be diminished. Even if creative talent has lain dormant, you can resurrect it through training and reinforcement. Often, you just have to let it out of the bottle. People have sometimes viewed creativity, like virtue, as its own reward. Certainly the intrinsic rewards that come from the satisfaction of accomplishment that accompanies a creative insight are powerful. Yet creative individuals, from scientists to toddlers, respond to extrinsic reinforcement as well.

Creative individuals need and respond to recognition, praise, and rewards. Consider, for example, that very few novels and even fewer (if any) scientific articles are published anonymously; composers copyright their music; artists sign their works.

Creative results are seldom anonymous.

Much of the world's great art, sculpture, and music have been produced on commission, as have many of the world's commercial innovations. Commissions not only provide monetary incentives, but they also facilitate innovation by setting clear goals that clarify expectations and deadlines for what is to be produced and when it is to be completed. Massive efforts in technological innovation and creativity grew out of President Kennedy's 1960 goal of putting a man on the moon by 1970. Mozart finished one of the world's greatest operas by working through the night preceding its premiere. In many fields, time pressures can be outrageous and productive. It has been said that creative people in advertising work best while "under the gun." Deadlines and creativity are not necessarily in conflict.

Of course, the imposition of tight deadlines can be carried too far and can force acceptance of the first creative response. Evidence abounds that conscious efforts to avoid the immediate acceptance of "first" solutions can enhance creative effort. In several studies, groups worked on problems until they arrived at a solution. They were then instructed to put that solution aside and to derive a second one. Invariably the second solutions were superior to the first, more conventional ones.

Individuals must be free to create. However, freedom and autonomy can be interpreted in vastly different ways. Certainly freedom from ridicule and fear is important, as are the opportunity and time to engage in preparation, incubation, reflection, and other elements of the creative process. Yet freedom and autonomy do not necessarily mean abandoning guidelines or constraints. Contrary to popular belief, creative individuals can live within budgets. One report analyzed 567 technical innovations in products or processes that occurred in 121 companies in 5 manufacturing industries. More than two-thirds of the innovations cost less than $100,000; only 2 percent cost over $1 million. Individuals with complete freedom seldom get on the track to creativity. In your projects, setting goals, budgets, and guidelines will facilitate rather than hinder the creative process, when people know that you and the project are counting on them. With the *what* is to be accomplished made clear, the freedom and creativity are focused on how to get the job done.

Deadlines and creativity are not necessarily in conflict.

To apply these ideas to projects, it is clear that projects with defined goals and objectives plus realistic deadlines will aid creativity and innovation. Thus, the **GOCART-S** process can actually enhance creativity, while also providing a structure to guide team member efforts. The maxim "Necessity is the mother of invention" rings true. Project personnel who do not know what is necessary seldom find creative and innovative solutions to problems. Successful high-technology firms encourage their product development engineers to get out into the field. Unless they do, there is a danger that Marketing's identification of an opportunity will not translate down to the product development engineers in a way they can appreciate.

Similarly, when you support your project team and tolerate risk tak-ing (and even failure), you develop a climate in which high levels of cre-ativity and innovation abound. Studies of managers who achieved extraordinary results in their organizations point out that people must be willing to challenge the process. Those who want everything to be right the first time will never take the risk of innovating.

Creative behavior deals in uncertainty, which requires support and frequent communication at the interpersonal level. Open exchanges of information and exposure to new ideas foster creative efforts. New prod-uct ideas need to be given time to germinate into a productive idea. Don't judge too quickly, and for sure don't give up on an idea before it has time to be considered from many different angles and with numerous options for application.

In addition, evidence demonstrates that both flexibility and diversity have positive impacts on creativity and innovation. Diversity promotes unique and sometimes dramatically different ideas, while flexibility per-mits the relatively easy adoption of new and different ways of doing things. Project teams should be and often are made up of individuals from diverse backgrounds and different specialties. If you as project leader allow it, this diversity can stimulate creative productivity by providing people with opportunities to come up with new combinations and associ-ations of ideas.

Like almost any desired behavior, creativity must be identified, actively encouraged, recognized, rewarded, and used. Your challenge is to exercise sensitivity about how to best provide reinforcement, goals, and deadlines, plus a measure of freedom and autonomy in order to encour-age creativity. Would the ark have ever been built on time or all the ani-mals assembled two by two if Noah had wanted to approve every decision that was made? Clarity about the project goal releases people's energies to pursue their tasks with enthusiasm and to accomplish astonishing results. Give people on the team information, goals, and deadlines, and then get out of the way to let their creativity take over!

Developing Better Ideas for Your Projects

To elicit the best ideas from your team, you have to believe and act as if everyone has the potential to be creative! Keep this in mind when projects bog down and get out of sync or when a timely, innovative solution is required to a difficult problem. At such times, you can act to either inhibit or facilitate creative expressions.

To avoid inhibiting creativity, be on guard for the myriad "killer phrases" that crop up and tend to dampen creative energies. Phrases like these will kill creativity: "We tried that before." "That'll never work." "It will cost too much." And "Let's not move too fast on that decision." When pushed to their logical extremes these phrases are illogical. Like any new seedling, an idea needs space, nourishment, and care until it can stand on its own. Killer phrases stomp on these ideas prematurely. So to the killer phrase statement, "But it's not in the budget!" you might respond "Of course not; we didn't have this idea when the budget was initially proposed," or "Do you mean to say that this organization won't support new ideas?" To the naysayers who exclaim, "We tried that before!" explain to them that "Now is different, in the following ways . . . ."

Being creative is within everyone's capability.

Better ideas can be developed through efforts to improve your ability and those of others in the following four areas:

1. Sensitivity to problems

2. Originality

3. Idea fluency

4. Flexibility

1. **Problem sensitivity** is the ability to recognize that a problem exists—to cut through misunderstanding, lack of facts, misconceptions, and other obscuring obstacles so that you perceive the real problem. To be a problem finder, not just a problem solver, requires you to be sensitive to early warning signs and potential red flags in the project life cycle. These signs and flags can warn you that your project is starting to veer off course or that it may be headed off a cliff. In being creative, it is important not to assume constraints that don't exist. Equally important is that assumptions are frequently reevaluated as information changes and time passes.

    The most frequent reason for problem insensitivity is that we place imaginary restraints on problems. The famous Nine-Dot puzzle in

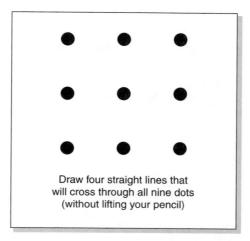

Draw four straight lines that
will cross through all nine dots
(without lifting your pencil)

Figure 10.1 An Example of Problem Insensitivity

Figure 10.1 demonstrates this point. The problem requires us to draw four straight lines through all nine dots without retracing and without lifting your pencil from the paper. This can also be done with only three lines, two lines, and even one line! Try this puzzle for a moment or two (we'll come back to the problem shortly).

What keeps many people from solving this problem immediately is a nonexistent constraint (or boundary) that they place on the problem. They assume they cannot draw lines outside an imaginary box defined by the eight dots that surround the center dot. Developing better ideas often requires you to test your assumptions, to go beyond your experiences (in this case to go outside the imaginary boundary), and possibly to bend the rules. In highly innovative organizations, people are apt to believe that "It's more fun to be a pirate than to join the Navy!"

2. **Originality** can take many perspectives. In practical, day-to-day problem solving, complete newness or pure originality is usually not what you need. The originality you require is more likely to be that of finding new ways to vary existing conditions, new ways to adapt existing ideas to new conditions, or a new modification of something to fit an existing condition. Conditions that impede originality include stereotypes, saturation, and failure to use all of our sensory inputs.

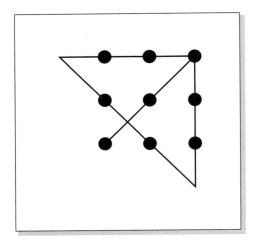

Figure 10.2 Going Outside the Boundaries Solves the Nine-Dot Problem

Stereotyping is to some extent the difficulty people have in the Nine-Dot problem. We see a square even when one is not intended. Imagination is limited by our tendency to see what we expect to see. As you may have determined, the solution to the Nine-Dot problem is to go outside the self-imposed, imaginary boundary, as shown in Figure 10.2.

Another factor that limits our ability to be original is called saturation. The more familiar we are with a situation (person, problem), the harder it is for us to see it in another context. Our tendency is to see all problems alike or to see all problems through a single filter (such as engineering, accounting, or public relations). For example, look at the list of numbers in Figure 10.3. See if you can determine the logic behind their particular sequence.

18, 11, 15, 14, 30, 12, 20

What is the logic behind this particular
sequencing of numbers?

Figure 10.3 An Example of Saturation

Difficult? The vast majority of people approach this problem as a "numbers" or mathematical problem because that's the form in which they found it. There is no easy numbers solution (if one is even possible!). But if you write out these numbers (for example, 18 becomes eighteen, 11 becomes eleven, 15 becomes fifteen), the solution becomes immediately apparent. Try it. It is clear that the numbers are in alphabetical order.

Too often we approach problems from a particular point of view, or stereotype, that limits our creative problem-solving ability. It also boxes people and departments in and limits their potential contributions, as in "Engineers can't talk with real customers," "Salespeople are more concerned about their customers than they are about this company," or "The accounting department always says no."

You also enrich your problem-solving ability when you use inputs from all of your senses. Visualization seems especially important. Friedrich Kekule, the famous chemist who discovered the structure of the benzene ring, did so in a dream after having devoted considerable conscious thought to its enigmatic structure. A delightful children's book is entitled *Put Your Mother on the Ceiling.* Children visualize this quite easily and naturally. It is this same skill that enables an architect to imagine what a building will look like when completed and how people will feel as they stroll through its lobby. It also allows a computer programmer to write user-friendly software, or the personnel specialist to design stimulating recruitment strategies, or Noah to prepare an ark for The Great Flood.

3. **Idea fluency** is the ability to generate a large number of alternative solutions to a problem in a given amount of time. It is the law of large numbers, from statistical theory, applied to problem solving. In other words, the more ideas you generate, the higher the probability that you will have one or more good ideas.

In a classical brainstorming sense, you need to separate idea generation from idea evaluation. Premature evaluation stops the generation of new ideas. Scholars of innovation have demonstrated quite persuasively that few ideas (concepts, processes, products) are immediate commercial successes. Night lighting for outdoor sports stadiums was several steps removed from the creation of iridescent lighting for ships at sea, and permeable face masks for coal miners were not the original intent of the inventors of disposable brassieres. Noah obviously asked for as many ideas as possible for determining the gender of porcupines before just trying to pick one up.

4. **Flexibility** is the willingness to eventually adopt a wide variety of approaches to a problem (for example, the interests of all parties involved). Rather than zeroing in on a particular idea, technique, or viewpoint that you like, you should start out by remembering that if one solution won't work, the problem can always be approached from another angle. Occasionally this requires a healthy skepticism about the obvious and a willingness to change (be flexible). As noted earlier, a group's first solution to a problem is generally less optimal than their second solution. You may have to push your project team to generate that second solution or challenge them to go beyond the initial solution.

   Flexibility is akin to idea fluency in asking you to view and understand a problem in different ways. But it goes further in that it means adopting an idea that may seem somewhat foreign to you or others on the team. What is the customer's viewpoint? How would this problem be perceived in the budget office? On the manufacturing floor? In the corporate boardroom? In the trade magazines?

   Consider the case of the project engineer who was called to the building superintendent's office. The superintendent said that many complaints had been received about the elevators being too slow, and she wanted the engineer to solve this problem. What would you do?

   A week passed, and the engineer announced he had a solution. The superintendent was delighted and expected to hear suggestions about increasing elevator speed, hydraulics, a new algorithm for sequencing the elevators during peak hours, or something similar. Instead the engineer proposed the installation of mirrors on each floor next to the elevators. If people were kept busy checking their appearance, he explained, they would have less time to notice the wait!

The boss had seen the problem as one of speeding up the elevators, but the engineer looked at the problem with flexibility. He chose to attack the impatience of the people waiting rather than the speed of the elevators. By failing to look at problems from different (multiple) perspectives, you often limit your creative potential.

Risk creative approaches to problems, and you
will be amazed at what your team can do!

In closing this chapter, let us note that had Noah not rewarded risk taking and encouraged creativity, he could not have succeeded in building, launching, and navigating the ark. Bringing your **GOCART-S** to the finish line for the checkered flag will require some degree of ingenuity. The most stimulating and rewarding projects are somewhat like racing on a road track, never really knowing for sure where the dips, twists, and turns are but enjoying the challenge and being confident in your ability to stay on course for the checkered flag.

Summary

Rule Ten:
Risk Being Creative

1. Contrary to what many people believe, creativity can be taught to people.

2. Before people on your project team can allow themselves to be creative, you have to eliminate potential blocks to risk taking.

3. Goals and deadlines can actually help to foster creativity, as do reinforcement and guided freedom.

4. Four strategies to encourage creativity are (1) increased sensitivity to problems, (2) originality, (3) idea fluency, and (4) greater flexibility.

G	Develop an Empowered Project Team
O	Reinforce Motivation and Energy
C	Inform Everyone Regularly
A	Vitalize with Energy from Conflicts
R	Empower Yourself and Others
T	Risk Being Creative
S	

Driving
to the
Checkered
Flag

Now you have ten proven rules for getting to the checkered flag on your projects! Plan and manage your projects by these ten rules, and you will be getting projects done on time, within budget, and with high quality. The primary reason lies in the integrative power of these ten rules. Throughout the development of the **GOCART-S** and the application of the **DRIVER** skills, you will be integrating the best of technology with people's abilities, and from this interaction comes the incredible magic for project victory.

Actively and fully applying the first four rules, you and your team will develop a sound plan for the project: a plan that inspires passion and energy from everyone on the project team to accomplish a well defined goal. The plan will be both clear to all team members and bought into by everyone, yet flexible enough to handle the unexpected and inevitable problems. It will be a plan that your team members can commit themselves to with both knowledge and passion. Your **S**upercharged **GOCART** will be capable of carrying you to the coveted checkered flag.

Then as you move through the project plan with the team, application of the last six rules will help you successfully manage the project plan through to completion. The **DRIVER** skills will enable you and the team to anticipate problems before they become severe enough to knock your **GOCART** out of the race. You will minimize unexpected pit stops, and your team will handle unexpected problems more effectively. You will recognize and seize opportunities to move ahead, because you will be navigating the course as a **DRIVER** who is well prepared and working with a team that is highly motivated to bring home the checkered flag.

Our bias for getting projects done on time, within budget, and with high quality is clear. By going slow at first, taking the time to develop your **GOCART-S**, you and the team will be able to speed to the finish line. Take the time to involve as many people as possible in building a complete and thoroughly designed **GOCART**. Then **S**upercharge it with a picture for real power. The payoff is quite clear, so take the time to:

Clarify the project **Goal**

Use **Objectives** to define responsibilities

Establish **Checkpoints** to monitor progress

Establish **Activities** to be completed

Clarify **Relationships** among the activities

Set **Time estimates** for the activities

Supercharge the plan with a picture

With the plan well defined and agreed to by everyone involved, manage the plan with the strength of your **DRIVER** skills. Continually work to refine, strengthen, and use your abilities as a **DRIVER** so that project implementation goes smoothly. Remember to:

Develop an empowered project team

Reinforce people's motivation and energy

Inform everyone regularly

Vitalize people with energy from conflicts

Empower yourself and others

Risk being creative

These are the ten rules followed by successful project leaders. Planning and managing projects is very challenging but also offers a great opportunity to be a winner. Practice these rules to more easily plan and implement projects and to increase the likelihood of victory. And remember:

GOCART (Supercharged) + **DRIVER** = Winning Project

Now the only thing left is for you to begin using these ten rules. If you do, we are confident you will see the checkered flag even more often. Good luck and "start your engines"!

References

Managing Projects: Challenge and Opportunity

Robert C. Ford and W. Alan Randolph. 1998. "Organizational Structure and Project Management." In Jeffrey K. Pinto. 1998. *Project Management Handbook*, pp. 88-106. San Francisco: Jossey-Bass Publishers.

Thomas L. Friedman. 2000. *The Lexus and the Olive Tree*. New York: Anchor Books.

Tom Peters. 2000. *The Project 50* (see the Introduction). New York: Alfred A. Knopf, Inc.

Rule One: Clarify the Project Goal

Ken Blanchard, John P. Carlos, and Alan Randolph. 2001. *Empowerment Takes More Than a Minute*, 2nd ed. (see the section on Create Autonomy Through Boundaries). San Francisco: Berrett-Koehler Publishers.

Ken Blanchard and Spencer Johnson. 1982. *The One Minute Manager* (see the section titled "One Minute Goals"). New York: William Morrow.

W. Alan Randolph. 2000. "Re-thinking Empowerment: Why Is It So Hard to Achieve?" *Organizational Dynamics*, Vol. 29, No. 2, pp. 94-107.

Rule Two: Objectives Define Responsibilities

Robert B. Angus, Norman A. Gundersen, and Thomas P. Cullinane. 2000. *Planning, Performing, and Controlling Projects* (see Appendix B). Upper Saddle River, NJ: Prentice Hall.

Robert Blonchek and Martin O'Neill. 1999. *Act Like an Owner.* New York: John Wiley & Sons, Inc.

Steven Kerr. 1975. "On the Folly of Rewarding A, While Hoping for B." *Academy of Management Journal.* Vol. 18, pp. 769-783.

Rule Three: Establish Checkpoints, Activities, Relationships, and Time Estimates

Sunny Baker and Kim Baker. 1998. *The Complete Idiot's Guide to Project Management* (see Part 3: The Project Planning Phase). New York: Alpha Books.

Ken Blanchard and Robert Lorber. 1984. *Putting the One Minute Manager to Work.* New York: William Morrow.

Tom Peters. 2000. *The Project 50* (see the sections on Create and Sell). New York: Alfred A. Knopf, Inc.

Rule Four: Supercharge the Plan with a Picture

Robert B. Angus, Norman A. Gundersen, and Thomas P. Cullinane. 2000. *Planning, Performing, and Controlling Projects* (see Chapter 7, "The Project Plan"). Upper Saddle River, NJ: Prentice Hall.

Jack R. Meredith and Samuel J. Mantel, Jr. 2000. *Project Management: A Managerial Approach*, 4th ed. (see Chapter 8, "Scheduling"). New York: John Wiley & Sons, Inc.

For information on Project Management software, check out the bookstore and "PM software" at the Project Management Institute's Web site, www.pmi.org.

Rule Five: Develop an Empowered Team

Ken Blanchard, Donald Carew, and Eunice Parisi-Carew. 2000. *The One Minute Manager Builds High Performing Teams*. New York: William Morrow.

Ken Blanchard, John P. Carlos, Alan Randolph, and Peter B. Grazier. 2000. *Power Up for Team Results*. San Francisco: Berrett-Koehler Publishers.

Russ Forrester and Allan B. Drexler. 1999. "A Model for Team-based Organization Performance." *Academy of Management Executive*, Vol. 13, No. 3, pp. 36-49.

Barry Z. Posner and James M. Kouzes. 1998. "The Project Manager." In Jeffrey K. Pinto. 1998. *Project Management Handbook*, pp. 249-255. San Francisco: Jossey-Bass Publishers.

Rule Six: Reinforce People's Motivation and Energy

Ken Blanchard and Spencer Johnson. 1982. *The One Minute Manager* (see the section on One Minute Praisings). New York: William Morrow.

James M. Kouzes and Barry Z. Posner. 1999. *Encouraging the Heart.* San Francisco: Jossey-Bass Publishers.

Gary N. Powell and Barry Z. Posner. 1984. "Excitement and Commitment: Keys to Project Success." *Project Management Journal,* Vol. 15, No. 4, pp. 39-46.

Rule Seven: Inform Everyone with Regularity

Sunny Baker and Kim Baker. 1998. *The Complete Idiot's Guide to Project Management* (see Chapters 19, 20). New York: Alpha Books.

R. G. Ghattas and Sandra L. McKee. 2001. *Practical Project Management* (see Chapter 4). Upper Saddle River, NJ: Prentice Hall.

Tom Peters. 2000. *The Project 50* (see the section on Implementation). New York: Alfred A. Knopf, Inc.

Rule Eight: Vitalize with Energy from Conflicts

Sunny Baker and Kim Baker. 1998. *The Complete Idiot's Guide to Project Management* (see Chapter 22). New York: Alpha Books.

David F. Caldwell and Barry Z. Posner. 1998. "Project Leadership." In Jeffrey K. Pinto. 1998. *Project Management Handbook,* pp. 300-311. San Francisco: Jossey-Bass Publishers.

Thomas F. Crum. 1993. *The Magic of Conflict Workbook: Your Personal Guidance System.* Aspen, CO: Aiki Works.

Jack R. Meredith and Samuel J. Mantel, Jr. 2000. *Project Management: A Managerial Approach,* 4th ed. (see Chapter 6, "Conflict and Negotiation"). New York: John Wiley & Sons, Inc.

Barry Z. Posner. 1986. "What's All the Fighting about in Project Management?" *IEEE Transactions in Engineering Management*, Vol. 33, No. 4, pp. 207-211.

Rule Nine: Empower Yourself and Others

Ken Blanchard, John P. Carlos, and Alan Randolph. 1999. *The 3 Keys to Empowerment: Release the Power within People for Astonishing Results.* San Francisco: Berrett-Koehler Publishers.

James M. Kouzes and Barry Z. Posner. 2002. *The Leadership Challenge,* 3rd ed. (see Chapters 2, 7, and 8). San Francisco: Jossey-Bass Publishers.

Charles C. Manz and Henry P. Sims, Jr. 2001. *The New Superleadership.* San Francisco: Berrett-Koehler Publishers.

Gary Yukl. 1997. *Leadership in Organizations,* 4th ed. Upper Saddle River, NJ: Prentice Hall.

Rule Ten: Risk Being Creative

Tom Peters. 2000. *The Project 50* (see the section on Implementation). New York: Alfred A. Knopf, Inc.

Roger von Oech. 1999. *A Whack on the Side of the Head: How You Can Be More Creative.* New York: Warner Books.

Rosamund Stone Zander and Benjamin Zander. 2000. *The Art of Possibility.* Boston, MA: Harvard Business School Press.

Index

The *Financial Times* delivers a world of business news.

Use the Risk-Free Trial Voucher below!

To stay ahead in today's business world you need to be well-informed on a daily basis. And not just on the national level. You need a news source that closely monitors the entire world of business, and then delivers it in a concise, quick-read format.

With the *Financial Times* you get the major stories from every region of the world. Reports found nowhere else. You get business, management, politics, economics, technology and more.

Now you can try the *Financial Times* for 4 weeks, absolutely risk free. And better yet, if you wish to continue receiving the *Financial Times* you'll get great savings off the regular subscription rate. Just use the voucher below.

8 reasons why you should read the Financial Times for 4 weeks RISK-FREE!

To help you stay current with significant
developments in the world economy ...
and to assist you to make informed business
decisions — the Financial Times brings you:

1 Fast, meaningful overviews of international affairs ... plus daily briefings on major world news.

2 Perceptive coverage of economic, business, financial and political developments with special focus on emerging markets.

3 More international business news than any other publication.

4 Sophisticated financial analysis and commentary on world market activity plus stock quotes from over 30 countries.

5 Reports on international companies and a section on global investing.

6 Specialized pages on management, marketing, advertising and technological innovations from all parts of the world.

7 Highly valued single-topic special reports (over 200 annually) on countries, industries, investment opportunities, technology and more.

8 The Saturday Weekend FT section — a globetrotter's guide to leisure-time activities around the world: the arts, fine dining, travel, sports and more.

For Special Offer See Over

FT FINANCIAL TIMES
World business newspaper

Where to find tomorrow's best business and technology ideas. TODAY.

- Ideas for defining tomorrow's competitive strategies — and executing them.

- Ideas that reflect a profound understanding of today's global business realities.

- Ideas that will help you achieve unprecedented customer and enterprise value.

- Ideas that illuminate the powerful new connections between business and technology.

ONE PUBLISHER.
Financial Times Prentice Hall.

FINANCIAL TIMES
Prentice Hall

WORLD BUSINESS PUBLISHER

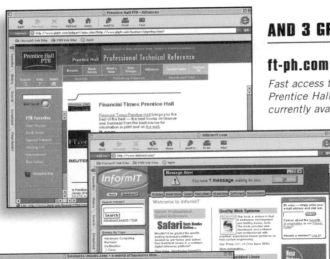

AND 3 GREAT WEB SITES:

ft-ph.com
Fast access to all Financial Times Prentice Hall business books currently available.

InformIt.com
Your link to today's top business and technology experts: new content, practical solutions, and the world's best online training.

Business-minds.com
Where the thought leaders of the business world gather to share key ideas, techniques, resources — and inspiration.